N
A
K
E
D

Owerri, Nigeria

N A K E D

A Journey To Self

ESE ARK

2016
Naira Books & Press

NAKED

Naira Books & Press
Plot 35A Block C2 [LIS]
Industrial Layout, Onitsha Road
Owerri, Imo State, Nigeria
08169241136
www.NairaBooks.com.ng

ISBN –978-978-54413-7-6

Printed and Bound By **Naira Books & Press Inc.**, *Owerri, Nigeria.*

DEDICATION

This book is dedicated to myself for sticking with me ☺

TABLE OF CONTENTS

INTRODUCTION

I am Ese.

Ese is the short version of Eseoghene, which translates directly to 'gift from god'.

My last name has changed through the years. It started off as Rugbere. I answered to this name through primary school and a portion of my secondary school years, which was when I developed a sense of self-consciousness around it. You see, I have a linguistic snag that makes me unable to properly pronounce the letter 'r'. Rugbere had two of those in it so it was quite the hassle. I would pronounce it as "wugbewe" and would have to spell and write it out to avoid re-naming myself whilst telling teachers and colleagues my name. After months of this embarrassment, I decided it was time to adopt a name that was no trouble.

Walter.

My dad's first name. I liked the sound of it. Two syllables, no Rs, very direct. And so, Ese Walter it was, up until two years after our marriage when I decided I was going to adopt my husband's last name – Ark.

My name is Ese Ark, and the journey of my name has been like the journey of my life. An evolution.

For almost three decades I practically sleepwalked through life. But I eventually got awakened during a period of my life that turned out to be the most interesting and challenging.

In the following pages are stories of my life's experiences from sleeping walking to awakening. My life is not over, so the journey is still ongoing, being exactly all that it needs to be at every start, stop, and intersection.

I have found my purpose and I am quite conscious of how this purpose impacts my world. I think that this can be your story too – you can awaken your world in all the areas where you may be 'asleep' even if unbeknownst to you. So if you allow me, it would be my pleasure to suggest new possibilities to you, and possibly show you a new vista, as I share my journey with you.

Love, and light

- Ese Ark.

1

BIRTH – Two Sides Of A Mysterious Coin.

"The two most important days in your life are the day you are born and the day you find out why."

— Mark Twain

I am told that I was born on the 29th of March 1984. It was a Thursday. Despite my curiosity about what happened in the weeks, days, hours and moments leading up to my birth, I have decided to accept and stay with the general details of my birth story, because I don't remember being born. I know no one who does. I therefore like to retell what I was told about my birth with a pinch of salt because what if I'm wrong? What if somebody forgot some important detail? What if the dates were mixed up or I was switched at birth?

I know why I was born. I know why I was created. I know why I have appeared in physical form on the earth at this time. I don't remember the exact moment I found out, and my knowledge of myself is in no way complete but I know that my life will not end when it ends in the physical form. Somehow, I will continue to 'be', but that should not and does not affect where I am in this physical form, now. In any case, birth for me is a very interesting subject. I see it as being not just about the child but also about the mother.

After carrying a baby for several months, getting to meet your baby should count as something of a 'rebirth' for mummy. Barring any mishaps and unforeseen problems, baby's birth-day is probably one of mummy's happiest days. So I like to imagine that there was a lot of happiness when I was born.

In a culture that promotes the birth of boys over

girls, I would not care to hear about any angst upon finding out I was a girl. I am the first child of my parents so the chances that they wanted a boy first are high, but I close my mind to the possibility that there might have been any disappointments. Still, I have often toyed with the idea of asking my parents deeper questions about my birth and their feelings surrounding it, but I have never gone ahead. It could end up feeling weird for all concerned. Also, I suspect some white lies might find their way in, giving false color to the story. You never know with these things.

By virtue of my birth date, my star sign is Aries. I am not an astute astrologist, but I am curious about anything that pertains to Ese and have read quite a bit about the characteristics of people born under the Aries sign. If you said that the traits of the Aries sign are the traits of Ese, you wouldn't be wrong. What's funny is that I started out reading about the Aries characteristic only for entertainment and as a way to fuel my wishful thinking. I however now study them as a reminder and validation of my characteristics and capabilities.

The earliest memory I have of a birthday party is when I was ten years old. Surely I had a one-year-old birthday celebration. I don't remember it though, which is why I didn't bother with a party when my son turned one. I don't think he would remember it. I was sure he would rather be in bed with his mummy, talking about "dada." I assume my own experience must have been something along those lines. Or maybe not. And if this is the case, I would not be shocked, because with me, things have always been somewhat different.

Asides from said birthday celebration, I do not remember a lot about growing up. This is probably because I have buried the past so far in my mind it disappeared, or maybe that science article was right about synoptic pruning and how it is possible to have an entirely new human being after a decade. Whatever the case, I neither remember nor have need for any story that is beyond my here and now.

I have a stepsister who was born in the same month and year as me. I didn't learn about her until I was eighteen, and even then, it took a few more years to hear about how her birth had affected the family. This aspect of our family life has often caused me to wonder what my own birth meant to my parents. Asides from the issue of male versus female children, was I 'wanted'? Was I not? Was I a sore reminder of someone else's poor decisions?

At birth, babies do not have a choice. They didn't ask to be born. In most cases, the mother is fully responsible for her choices. After birth, most mothers change physically, and even more, emotionally. I imagine my mother experienced this change too, but I haven't been privy to that story, neither have I dug for it.

I was told that I wasn't breastfed. My dear mother had to go back to school to finish her education while

I lived with my grandma. I hear my great grandma was alive and part of my life at the time but all these are stories that I don't remember experiencing. With all the talks about the importance of breastfeeding, I wonder sometimes if that affected my early development in any way. Could breastfeeding have saved me years of rebellion or created the special bond that seems to elude dear mother and I?

Was my birth special? Was I dedicated in a church? Did I ever fall on my head? Then again, was the Universe kind to the new mother who bore me? Did she feel joy or sadness? Seeing as postpartum depression is something that a lot of Nigerian mothers deny in the twenty-first century, is it possible that it was something anyone understood in the eighties?

When birth happens, the once pregnant woman is experiencing a change, a transition, just as the new life is experiencing the same. Did my mother know who she was, and who she became after having me? My birth story is not complete without hers and I hope that when I eventually prod, there will be newfound truths coming from her to aid the completion of the knowledge of who I am and who she is, for as a new mother births her baby, she also births herself.

2

FAMILY - Is Blood Thicker Than Water?

"Families are messy. Immortal families are eternally messy. Sometimes the best we can do is remind each other that we are related for better or for worse."

Rick Riordan.

One of my favorite scientists said that if we trace the lineage of every person alive today we will find that we are all related. We'd fine that our ancestors are the same. My question then became: what's with the division along lines of race, class, blood, and water?

I know we were taught that family is the small unit within which you are born but I think it goes beyond that. Small units are great but what happens to the people who don't have one of those? Are they without family?

I thought "blood is thicker than water" spoke to the strength of family over friendship, until somebody threw light on the statement and made me to look at it differently.

In the university, we had cults – fraternities and confraternities – and it was common knowledge that there were rituals conducted if you wanted to join any of those groups. Campus rumor had it that blood oaths were among some of the things that made up initiation rites. The members of the cult would make incisions on the fingers of the new entrants, drops of blood would be put in a bowl, which would in turn be passed around for everyone to sip.

It is my friend's belief that the cult 'brothers' were bound by blood. Siblings on the other hand are bound by 'water', because while in utero it was water that kept each child floating around. Blood being thicker than water therefore meant that a fellow cultist was closer to you than a sibling with whom you shared a womb. It made sense to me, in a roundabout sort of way. Plus, it explained what I always thought about family being bigger than the small units we were born into.

Like most humans on the earth, after my birth I was introduced to my family, my own small unit. As I grew, so did my small unit with mummy and daddy heading the direction of the rest of us. While I don't remember a lot of my childhood memories, I remember that I always felt a special connection with the ones I called siblings over the ones I called friends. It was as though the people in my small unit were my inner circle, the ones I could easily trust, and the ones who didn't have a choice but to love me. They were also the ones I could take for granted without worrying about repercussions.

I see now how small units can easily create a 'we vs. them' mentality. The people who didn't have a choice but to love me were the ones who were "my people" while the people who wouldn't put up with what they didn't have to were "the others." When we separate ourselves from others either by beliefs, causes, cults or DNA, we cause a divide. We create the 'we vs. them' prison.

If you do a little research into the history of the world you'd find that humans have committed the worst kinds of atrocities against other humans based on those divisions that are present in society.

Today, leaders of poor countries are known to send their 'families' to better parts of the world while the citizens feel the heat of under-development and decrepit amenities. They think that by protecting the small unit they are doing enough to protect themselves from the rest of the people. People steal billions of naira and hide these on behalf of their 'families' while other citizens starve to death. The fact that you can be unkind to some people because they are not family proves that you are an unkind person, and even your family should be afraid of you, because what if you were not related to them? You would not care if they died of hunger and that is a very scary prospect.

I have two younger brothers and two stepsisters. For a long time, I didn't know how to explain my family. I loved saying I was the first-born but that wasn't the full story. I am the third, right in the middle of two girls and two boys. And even though both girls weren't born by my mum, they are my family, my small unit, and by virtue of our own peculiar sub-divisions, we are five children from daddy and three from mummy.

When I got married, I could not bring myself to see my husband as my family. To my mind, it didn't make sense that this man who was a stranger a few years ago should suddenly become family. This was territory that was specially reserved for my parents and siblings, and so any time my husband and I had issues, I was quick to call my 'family' on him.

When we had our son, I thought I had finally gotten a hang of this family thing. I tried. I told myself every time that we were family. A father, mother and child (ren) is what we are taught family consists of. In the case of aunties, grannies and cousins, we called them extended family. And other people are friends and strangers.

I call my best friend my sister. When I call her that it doesn't seem different from my stepsisters and brothers. And what's with the step anyways? Isn't that another way of creating a division that shouldn't exist?

Somebody said 'you can choose your friends but you cannot choose your family.'

I think you can choose your family. You can convert friends to family and still get all the love and security you deserve. A lot of people say that friends have been more understanding in their most difficult times than traditional family. Plus, a lot of families have the worst fights and very terrible dynamics where people aren't speaking to each other for years because one or more individuals just cannot forgive a score. I have been there too, and my curiosity always leaned towards why it seems far easier to hold grudges with the people we call family than anyone else?

What's the special bond between fathers and daughters and mothers and sons? What's the 'beef' between most mothers and daughters? How can the people who swore to love each other till forever swear now that they hate each other? Is family what it used to be? Is it evolving? Can we evolve with it? What's the difference between you and the man on the street?

That last one is a real question. Think about it. Better yet, look at random people on the street as you go about your day and ask the question about difference. People are different because we say they are. And people are family because we say they are.

Family doesn't give anyone special privileges. Except when you are broke and need family to help. He he he. In those instances, the people we call family tend to lend more help than the others. At least it has been so in my experience.

By and large, I think we need to expand our idea of family and allow ourselves bring in 'strangers' into our world, whilst remembering that we are all connected, after all said and done.

I remain a strong believer in the notion that family is the whole of humanity. We are family and the earth is our home. It is our duty to protect our home and each other.

3

CULTURE –

Laws of The Land.

"Culture is the characteristics and knowledge of a particular group of people, defined by everything from language, religion, cuisine, social habits, music and arts. The Center for Advance Research on Language Acquisition goes a step further, defining culture as shared patterns of behaviors and interactions, cognitive constructs and understanding that are learned by socialization. Thus, it can be seen as the growth of a group identity fostered by social patterns unique to the group."- Livescience.com

Culture feels like a wider range of family units. In my case, being familiar with my culture promised an expanded sense of family. It meant I could belong to a larger unit than the one that consisted of my child and husband, or my parents and siblings. It meant I could be part of a large group of people I may never get to know personally. The opportunity to expand my small unit beyond the few people it consisted of sounded good to me.

In reality though, I didn't care very much for my culture. I didn't understand it and had no intention of learning anything about it. By being born into it there were some things that I naturally came to accept, but as I developed as a human being, something in me fought everything I had grown to know.

In therapy I was told that I did not behave within the context of my culture. Maybe there was some shame around what I thought my culture meant because the inner rebellious self never seemed to fit in.

Culture changes as it is passed from generation to generation. This is because human beings are the vehicles of culture. As the human being evolves, the nature of culture will continue to mold itself to suit each step in this evolutionary journey.

When I first became interested in my culture, the journey seemed very intriguing and a part of me wanted to learn more, to better understand and appreciate the essence of culture to my being. I thought that having a more intimate understanding of my culture would help me feel more like part of a group as opposed to feeling like a fish out of water. I wanted that, but sometimes I was not so certain.

Then I stumbled upon an article about the importance of cultural heritage. I learnt that culture gives people a connection to certain social values, religion, beliefs and customs. And isn't that one of the intrinsic needs of every human? Connection?

Also, despite my feelings around my culture I knew that it formed the foundation for a lot of my core beliefs. Culture influenced my religion, social values, beliefs, and to some extent music. Arts and crafts, food, religion, music, languages and clothing offered up rich heritage and it was all so beautiful and mind blowing. So how could anyone be uninterested? Why had I been hesitant to fully embrace everything it meant?

I found a culture heritage circle on cultureindevelopment.nl and it states that by UNDERSTANDING cultural heritage people value it, by VALUING it people want to care for it, by CARING for it, people enjoy it and from ENJOYING it people have a thirst to understand it.

In an article titled, "African Culture and the Ongoing Quest for Excellence," Maulana Karenga says, *"Our culture provides us with an ethos we must honor in both thought and practice. By ethos, we mean a people's self-understanding as well as its self-presentation in the world through its thought and practice in the other six areas of culture. It is above all a cultural challenge. For culture is here defined as the totality of thought and practice by which a people create, celebrate, sustain, develop and introduce itself to history and humanity."*

After reading this, I wanted to pick up every Nigerian culture book I could find and educate my mind. I wanted to be abreast of my culture. I wanted to understand, value, care for and enjoy it. I wanted to represent my rich heritage and introduce myself to the world as one who understood whom she is and where she was coming from. And at the same time, even without those books, something in me already knew, because by the simple fact of living and growing up in Nigeria, I was already acculturated before I was aware.

Perhaps this was why I always admired African crafts without needing a reason to, because whether I was accepting of my culture or not, my culture already chose and accepted me.

I see people who are in complete touch with their cultural heritage and I feel some shame. I remember how I once denied my culture and tried to inherit a foreign one. My justification was that the world was changing and developing and we had to develop with it. I thought my culture was an archaic notion requiring replacement by new cultures that represented the time I lived in.

I am learning that even though culture might change, there are parts of a people that will always long for it. That part of me is only now accepting that a big chunk of my culture already resides within me. Therefore, instead of fighting what is, I want to understand and find expressions for it before I die.

I call culture the laws of the land because they are the rules that don't need to be spoken. Being born into Nigerian culture, I know that elders like to be seen as wise, and they love to receive a display of respect from younger people. This was the hardest reconciliation for me to make when I lived in London. Many times my lecturer told me, *"my name is John, and you can call me that."* I always called him sir and it was strange to him. Calling my lecturer by his name was strange to me. As basic an example as that is, it spoke volumes to me. I was Nigerian; we don't call our lecturers by their names.

Barring any harmful cultural practices, which have to be examined and expunged, there was absolutely nothing wrong with my heritage. And this is where I am right now, a Nigerian, and fiercely proud of it.

4

SCHOOL – The Beginning of Groupthink.

"Everybody is a genius. But if you judge a fish by its ability to climb a tree, it will live its whole life believing that it is stupid." Albert Einstein.

They say when a child is born, he is like an empty recording-tape and for the first few years of life, he is learning by absorbing everything around him.

My first schooling experience was in Sokoto, and I used to speak Hausa fluently then. I still remember some of the school songs I learnt in Hausa. I must have absorbed all that Hausa without even trying.

I think of the infants and toddlers in crèche and how fast they learn by daily interaction with their teachers and classmates.

By primary school, the child is taught to sing National Anthems while standing still. Then the child is put in a class with others and asked to learn in a particular way while being tested on how well he can reproduce what he learnt.

The quote about the fish is credited to Einstein although there are arguments that he didn't say it. I couldn't find anyone else who said it so I have credited it to him.

When we think about the fish and how effortlessly it swims. It lives in water; that's its home. It could never climb a tree and it will be ridiculous to judge its ability by whether or not it can climb trees. It's a no brainer to judge its ability by whether or not it can swim. Leave the tree climbing to monkeys and other mammals.

It's the same thing that happens in schools. We put

different people together and force them to learn exactly the same way. We grade them by how fast they can learn and regurgitate what they have learnt, not minding that different people will naturally learn in different ways.

I didn't know how I learnt until law school. I didn't even know there were people who were visual learners. Do all Nigerian schools recognize this? Or is everyone expected to learn the exact same way and then compete for who can reproduce what they learnt the fastest and the best? Is that kind of competition fair? Is it normal? Should it be normal?

Why were we encouraged to hit the desk and echo a greeting every time a teacher or visitor walked into our class? What if we didn't feel like greeting or standing up? Why do teachers embarrass and even punish students for being different? Why is the different one the weird one? Is it possible for every member of a class to feel the exact same way about every situation?

School for me is the beginning of learning how to conform, rather than the freedom to follow a different path. It is where we make our first friends and find ways around how we are common and alike than different. When there is a protest in a school setting, many people who would normally not opt for a protest will find themselves in the crowd, placard in hand, screaming *"we nor go gree"*, even if they have no idea what they are disagreeing about.

School should be a place where a person learns 'how' to think, not 'what' to think. School should encourage individuality over group thinking. When people are better able to think for themselves they serve better in a group setting because then there will be diverse ideas that everyone can draw from.

I learnt plenty about life just by experiencing school. I didn't learn much about books though. I believed I was a slow student so I didn't bother tasking my brain to try and compete with the rest of my classmates. It was enough that I got from one level to the next.

I remember how I often tried to think like most of my friends. I tried to like what they liked and do what they did but I always felt resistance from my inner self. My worldview was far removed from most of their realities. My way was the different way, and it was generally regarded as the weird way. It was as though I had to be like everyone else to fit in and we know how important it is to fit in in school. Being a loner was unattractive, scary even.

In school, there were girls who formed cliques. They sat together, walked together, ate together and did most things together. I never liked these cliques. I had one friend and that was enough. I think cliques have a way of making every member feel they have to be a certain way, and for students, what better way to lose your individuality than to mimic a clique's code of conduct until it becomes your own?

We live in a world that is evolving. We live in a world

that is said to have been in existence for billions of years. The thing to do when a new human arrives earth side is to guide them as they figure what this life is about and what they want from it. Schools instead pitch students against each other, fostering a competitive mentality while stifling the questioner that's inherent in every single one of us.

When I started asking questions about life, I realized most of my schooling years were a blur. I don't remember much of what happened there. I don't even remember most of what I learnt. I do remember the many times I got in trouble though. And I certainly remember the boys. I enjoyed the company of boys a lot. Perhaps it had something to do with needing some difference. Boys were not like girls so it must have been refreshing to have that diversity in company.

After my Master's program, I knew I was done with formal education. I had gone on to do a Master's degree not because I was interested furthering my education, but because at the time I was confused about what I wanted to do with my life. I assumed that the time away would help me figure it out. It didn't.

School asked me what I wanted to be when I grow up. That's another way of asking what I wanted to do with my life. How does a child know? Can the thing you want to do or become change? Sure it can. Confusion arises when you say one thing and find yourself gravitating towards another thing.

I am now accepting that I may never know what I want to do with my life, at least not in its entirety. I am happy to evolve, loving the things that I love, doing the things that I love to do, discarding some, picking up others, and generally just 'becoming'.

Ponder on this. Your schoolmates are getting married and birthing babies but there you are still trying to figure life out. Many people will not own up to the fact that even with the babies, the family and white picket fences, they still don't know what they want for their lives. So everyone is likely to keep pretending that they have found who they are. Then the same competition you learnt in school will come up again. You start wondering why you can't seem to get your life together and be like the Joneses. It's the groupthink bug that got you. You're very likely unaware, and perhaps also afraid, to cut loose and chart your own course.

If anyone had taken time to let you know that it is okay to be different, that it is okay to not know, that it is okay to try to figure it out at your own pace, you would not feel as loosely connected as you do now.

If they had told you earlier on in life that this was not a competition and even if it were, the competition is always with yourself, maybe you would not have to deal with the depressive thoughts that seem to colour your days in the now.

While school fosters groupthink, as we evolve we have the capacity to break away from that and create our own paths. Those who live the most interesting lives are those who blaze their own trails and accept all of life as lessons. There can be no failure or mistakes, only feedback. Now that you know this, help a student figure this out early. So that together, we can save those who are coming after us from the confusion that we battled and are battling. It is possible.

5

GIRLS – Are We Cat Fighters?

"She was free in her wildness. She was a wanderess, a drop of free water. She belonged to no man and to no city." Roman Payne.

As young girls, what we wanted above anything else was to play and make friends. There was something comforting in having a friend or group of friends. We wanted to have fun as little girls and we still want to have fun as adults. The only difference is our definition of fun as adults has changed. The way we trust friends has changed, too.

On a personal note, as a young adult I didn't have a lot of female friends. It wasn't because of fear or trust issues. It was just what it was. I am now learning that even though I can be a sociable person, my more comfortable norm is anti-social. I'd rather stay home with cans of energy drinks, a strong Internet connection for YouTube videos, and plenty writing, than go out to party or hang with friends. So it would seem like my idea of fun has changed. Or maybe it was always like this and I could not properly own it because I didn't understand or accept why I felt differently than my friends did about socializing.

When I was 7 years old, my friend and her mum came visiting at my parent's house. I couldn't stop staring at my friend's hair, as it was shiny and straight. She had it packed in a band behind her ears and it looked so good. Her hair looked different from the last time I had seen it when it was nappy and short like mine. I felt jealous but I didn't say anything to my friend. I just quietly looked at her hair as we played. I also made my own plans as to how I was going to get my hair straight and shiny too.

That night after she left, I locked myself in the bathroom with a jar of baby jelly. I was determined to get my shine on. After putting more than half of the jar in my hair with no shine in view, I called my elder sister to rescue me. She was shocked at what I had done to my hair. She asked what I was trying to achieve and I told her about my friend's hair. She explained that my friend's hair was permed, but I didn't know what that meant at the time. I only understood that Vaseline wouldn't help me achieve the intended shine. I was disappointed and jealous.

I don't know if men have this petty jealousy going on, but I bet many women are familiar with it. There are women who support other women without jealousy, but it seems like it is more usual to be green with envy when a friend seems to be doing better than you.

Petty jealousy is unfortunately a common phenomenon amongst women. A friend gets a high-paying job and you feel weird about it. A friend kicks off her online business and your advice is *"don't be so optimistic, online businesses are hard to sustain."* A friend is getting married and you are pondering on how she managed to 'catch' a spouse while you are still single.

Something happened in my life that helped me shine the light on this female jealousy. I met this girl who wanted to be friends. Actually, she came into my life as some sort of savior. After having loads of drama in my life, I became open to meeting people who

I thought cared for me. It turned out this lady had ulterior motives. First, she was interested in a guy I dated briefly, who she believed hadn't gotten over me. Secondly, she thought I had gifts she could help me manage.

When I found out she wasn't entirely honest with me about how she had come into my space, I had a few red flags go off but I ignored them because I couldn't imagine why a stranger would be dishonest with me. We became business partners and I found that it was hard to work with her. I decided to terminate our business to save the friendship but she didn't understand it. She turned hostile and said a few hurtful things to me. Initially, I was confused and wondered what triggered that behavior in her. During this time, I also found out that she had been dishonest about the work she was doing for me. Work I paid for. I was hurt and disappointed. Then I grew angry and decided I was going to show her how bad I could be.

I made all these plans about how to get back at her and spoil her business with other clients but in the end it didn't feel right, and it certainly was not worth my time. So I let her go. I let all the hurt and disappointment go. I took all that happened as part of my life's experience. It was good that it happened because I could learn that sometimes you don't need to do anything bad to people for them to hate you. And they may not really hate you per se. It might just be that it is themselves they hate. There's a thing called projection. It drives most humans, and this could very well be what the problem is with people of this kind – people who seem to hate you for absolutely no cause.

I have also had wholesome relationships with women I call friends, and my best friend is a woman. I think that girls tend to have best friends more than boys. I am testament to the fact that girls can be best friends for as long as forever.

My best friend is Ezinne Ihekire. I call her Beld. I met her my first night on campus. She came to my room with her aunt who asked if her niece could spend the night in my room. They arrived campus after the school accommodation officer had closed for the day so Ezinne was kind of stranded. I, therefore, agreed to have her stay the night, but we were already two students in the room so she shared my bed.

The next morning, we were up early for our orientation processes. Law students were sent back to the hostel to wear clothes conforming to the law dress code (black and white) before entering the law department. Most of us went back to change and I noticed she didn't have any black and white outfit. I gave her one of mine. It was like how kids share their toys with other kids.

After orientation, I accompanied her to look for her room. Her room already had two students. The accommodation officer gave the room to another student because she wasn't available to claim it the day before.

We went to the accommodation office to complain and we were told that the room capacity was three students. Apparently, the students that year were more than the accommodation provided for. She was asked to join both girls to make up the numbers. However, she asked the accommodation officer if she could be allocated the third space in my room since she had spent the night there and we were course mates. She was then assigned to my room. A third bed couldn't fit in the room so we had to continue sharing my bed.

One day we were talking about how secondary school had bunkmates and they were called bunky.

"What do we call two people sharing a bed?"

"Bedy?"

She laughed. We started calling each other Bedy.

A few weeks later, we decided Bedy was too basic. We added an 'l' in the word and came up with Beldy, and then we shortened it to Beld. Every time we meet new people, they ask why we call each other the same name. And for those who have known us for any amount of time, they call us Beld, too.

She introduced me to alcohol. I liked it because it was sweet; I kept gulping it as she refilled my cup. I don't remember being tipsy; all I remember was hanging my head over the balcony in front of the room, throwing my guts up. She rubbed my back as she assured me that it was okay. I passed out a few minutes after we got back into the room.

The next morning, I had a hangover, but that evening, I had another drink, slower this time. And it went better than the last time. We shared many other experiences that bonded us over the years, and to say those were some of the most fun times of my life would be making an understatement.

Beld left university after our second year to continue her education in the United Kingdom. When she returned to Nigeria, it was as if she never left, and we are still best friends to this day. I trust her more than I have trusted any other person in my life. I think she is a constant reminder that even though 'jealousy' seems to be a norm between girls, we were not necessarily built to fight each other.

Despite the crazy experiences I have had with some females in my life, she reminds me that there are still good souls in the world. And I believe I do the same for her. She is testament to the fact that girls still want that person they can chit-chat with, that person they can cry with, be vulnerable with and sometimes gossip with, and that person doesn't have to be a lover or partner, just a friend who you are safe with. Beld is that person for me.

We have spent most of our adult lives living in different countries but it doesn't change anything. If there is something going on in my life that matters to me, she is the first person outside my family that knows about it. Sometimes even before my family.

6

BOYS – Am I Inferior to Them?

"Boys are beyond the range of anybody's sure understanding."

James Thurber.

I grew up thinking I was inferior to boys. I thought I was created to make a man happy, to serve him, to put my needs on hold to attend to his. I thought if a man wasn't happy with how I looked, how smart I sounded, or if he didn't think I was pretty enough, slim enough, or good enough, then I was doing something wrong.

In her book *Lean In*, Sheryl Sandberg writes about how girls quit work before they start. Usually, before a girl gets the job, she is already thinking about children and when she will quit work to have them. Sheryl was encouraging more girls to 'sit at the table', and I felt like she was talking directly to me.

I thought about the conversations I had with my friends. We'd talk about leaving work for at least ten years to take care of the children. We were nineteen. Why were we so focused on marriage at that age? Now, I imagine boys thinking about how they wanted to build empires and make billions, but we were more occupied with thoughts of being one of the things those billions could 'acquire'. For. The. Boys.

As a young adult, I had a lot of shame around sex. I couldn't talk freely about it or express desires to engage in it. While boys were bragging about all the sex they were not having, the girls were labeled 'bad' if they owned up to liking sex. Two adults (male and female) have consensual sex and somehow the woman is the whore and the man is the player.

If the girl is raised to think she has an expiry date so

she has to 'keep herself', and then hurry through life so as to raise as many minis as she can, and the boy is raised to think that he is meant to be served and can acquire as many women as he wants, then is there any surprise we are where we are today?

I also imagine that boys struggle with what's expected of them. When boys are born and forced into that 'man box,' no one asks them what they want or need. So, they show up in the world like superheroes with no superpowers.

They are taught to be providers, protectors, and 'macho' in the world. From a young age, boys and girls are taught that a girl is weak, and is meant to serve and pamper the men in her life. Why else would discussions about feminism in Nigeria often be reduced to the ability of a woman to cook a pot of soup? And why do some women live as though a man is the most important part of her existence?

It is not unheard of that most young girls are smarter than young boys their age, but as they grow, some girls will hide their intelligence so that a man somewhere is not intimidated.

When I started dating, I used to hide my intelligence when relating with boys especially if I liked them. Why was it important to me that the boys went away feeling smarter than I was? In school, boys were more confident in class while some girls, like me, would shy away from answering questions or sparking up classroom debates. Back then, it was enough for me that I knew the answer to a question, it didn't matter that I didn't raise my hand or say anything out loud. However, most boys would confidently scream out some random answer even when they were not sure it was right.

It wasn't until I started getting conscious of who I was that I realized how this inherent need to be helped and empowered, disempowered me in actuality. It made me think I needed a following of women to be able to stand in my truth. Women still have a long way to go but the answers we seek will not necessarily be found in groups or women supporters. The answers lie in the foundational aspects of home life. Until we begin to teach boys and girls the same lessons about respect, strength and honor, nothing will change.

Growing up, I heard I needed to be in the kitchen to learn how to cook for my future husband. My brothers on the other hand didn't need to learn to cook. Somewhere in the universe, another mother was training her girls to cook for them. It felt like I was being trained to take care of a man's tummy. It was disconcerting, but it was what I was being fed and I knew no different way. In fact, god forbid a woman didn't know how to cook; you would hear people say things like, "who will marry her?"

All around me, teenage girls who had not decided what they wanted to do with their lives, already 'knew' how important it was to be able to cook for a man.

If this didn't scream inferior, then what would? And

it didn't stop there. As I interacted with others girls, I learned I wasn't alone in this "learn to cook for him" grill. Girls around Nigeria can get together and exchange notes on how they were taught to be inferior to men, in many ways.

When it comes to marriage, in many cultures, the man is expected to pay a 'bride price', the definition of which is still a hot topic of debate across various fora. But looking at the term in its simple meaning, what imagery is conveyed when one speaks of a 'price'? No matter how it is decorated, the fact remains that when a man pays a 'price', he is 'buying' the woman from her family.

I hear some families use this as an opportunity to milk the man for money. And even if not, if he is buying a woman for no matter how small the amount, is it any surprise he sees her as property? Should we raise an alarm when he starts to use her as a punching bag? Or when he decides to kick her out for a 'newer model'?

How about when a couple cannot get pregnant and the woman is immediately termed barren. She has to prove she was a good girl who did not 'commit' several abortions that ended up destroying her womb. Most times she does this convincing by overcompensating, overlooking areas in which she is being mistreated, and generally kowtowing to the wishes of judgmental members of her husband's family. Anything contrary, and not only is she 'barren', but she is probably a 'witch' as well, because she has not met up to the expectations that society has set for her gender, in 'pleasing' the man and/or completing his 'family' picture.

Am I inferior to boys? I vote no. I don't feel inferior to boys and I don't focus on anything that tells me I am. Misogynistic men and women-empowering movements serve the same purpose, for me. The empowering groups remind me that my gender is inferior and needs help. I don't think a woman needs help anymore that a man does. Just because more women hold meetings to talk about their problems doesn't mean the perceived problem is all there is.

Men and women are both victim and villain in this thing called life. None is inferior or superior to the other. Think about it this way: if women were inferior, would they need constant reminding of that? Doesn't the constant reminding serve as programming to keep us projecting inferior? And what are some boys really afraid of that they need to beat, threaten, manipulate and control women? Do they even know?

7

SEX – Is It Overrated?

"The major civilizing force in the world is not religion, it is sex."

Hugh Hefner.

I don't remember a lot about the first time I had sex. Which is weird because I was ready for it. What I do remember though, is that I had been looking forward to the day and when it finally happened I wasn't pleased.

#Bringbackmyvirginity.

After it happened, I was so upset that I wished I could undo it and remain a virgin but it was too late. Subsequent times, sex seemed like it was more about the other person than it was about me. It took a while to sort out how I felt about the whole thing and I even went as far as claiming I loved sex for a long time until I realized I really wasn't the sex machine I portrayed. My seeming appetite for sex was created to make a boyfriend think he was the best sex I ever had. I also didn't want him going to get it elsewhere so I was ever ready to serve. It's a type of people-pleasing. If I have more sex with him he will love me more and stay with me. It was desperate and fake.

I had a lot of sex as a young adult. Sometimes I had sex because I wanted to, but other times I had sex because someone else wanted to or it felt like the right thing to do at the time. I also didn't attach a lot to sex. Most guys I had sex with told me they thought my detachment was weird, yet some guys were attracted to it. I couldn't figure what the big deal about sex was, and why girls had to treasure the first time. After all, logically, there's a first time for everything, right? So what was the fuss about?

The general message we heard about sex didn't help either. Adverts, music videos, movies and everything on screen told us how great sex was. If you were not having any, you would think you were missing out on something earthmoving. If you were having some, you would be led into thinking you weren't having enough or maybe you were having it with the wrong person.

Boys and girls tend to feel different types of pressure when it comes to sex. The boy has to act like he is getting it every day, everywhere, while the girl has to act like she has had it once in a lifetime, feels apologetic about that one time, and will only continue to have sex within the 'holy' enclave of marriage.

A friend told me her husband asked her how many guys she had been with and she told him he was her third. We both laughed as she said that. It reminded me of a time a boyfriend asked me how many guys I had been with and I gave him an actual figure after doing a mental calculation. For the next week he kept telling me he couldn't believe I had been with all those people. It made me wonder why I didn't lie to him.

With the number of humans on the planet, it's safe to assume that a lot of sexing is going on. In the same light, there are a lot of people who aren't having half the sex they should be having. We have built shame around sex to the point that a young person cannot buy a pack of condoms in a pharmacy without feeling judged by the baleful stares and eyebrows raised in curiosity.

This also causes our sexual education to suffer. A lot of women my age got the same type of sex education growing up. *"Don't do it or you will get pregnant and disgrace the family"* was pretty much what most of us heard. So when we had sex and didn't get pregnant, we thought somebody lied.

I have stopped deluding myself that everybody is having sex. Everybody is not having sex. Some will remain virgins until they get married and the 'baddest' player on the block may not be getting any sex at all. I also do not think a person needs another person in order to have an orgasm. There are toys people use to pleasure themselves and I have stopped judging those. Even though everyone might not be having sex, it is my firm belief that everyone is entitled to a regular orgasm and if they are going to get it by self-help, I'm going to root for them, because orgasms are important.

I think there's a link between orgasms and creativity. My friend even says the same energy field drives sex and creativity. So for instance, it is not uncommon that orgasms can give one a creative burst. Who doesn't want that? I certainly do. So I rank orgasms high above sex because you can have the all-important big-O without the much raved about act of sex which comes with a lot of pressure and unrealistic expectations.

Therefore, at the risk of playing down sex, I think it is overrated in our world. We need to get to a point where we are honest about our need for it or the lack thereof, and stop painting misleading pictures.

It is not that deep! No pun intended.

8

MONEY –
Does It Make You Happy?

"Money has never made man happy, nor will it; there is nothing in its nature to produce happiness. The more one has, the more one wants."

Benjamin Franklin.

I used to think money was evil. I don't remember where I absorbed such a notion from but I believed it was bad and everyone who had a lot of it was depriving everybody else and was therefore evil. I didn't like anything that involved a lot of money. I didn't know how to have a good time because I believed it made me evil to enjoy myself while some people somewhere were not having such a fine time. I convinced myself that I didn't like big cars, big houses, nice cloths and bags, travel and vacations at choice locations. I thought it made me humble to think small, be small and expect small from life.

The first time I had an opportunity to think about my relationship with money was after I listened to a business podcast where money was the subject. The speaker said that in order to understand how she related with money she had to think back to her early experiences with it. She grew up with a dad who said money was bad and she accepted this, but as an adult this kind of thinking was crippling her in no small way.

I started thinking about my own relationship with money. I was always afraid that money would never be enough. I remember growing up and hearing my mum talk about the need to save money. I had this weird dance going on with money where I didn't save. Even when I was not earning, I was more inclined to spend money like someone who had a lot of it. I just had no value for money, so I let it go out of my hands faster than it came in.

Nobody understood it and when anyone tried to talk to me about my attitude towards money, I would interpret it as an attack on my person and would then proceed to hotly defend my right to be broke.

Even when I would have some money, I would spend all of it to maintain that belief that it wasn't enough. It was an unconscious action that took me a while to realize let alone attempt to understand. It didn't matter how much I had in the bank, if it wasn't spent to the last dime, I would feel wrong about myself.

The second time I had an opportunity to think about money and how to make some, I had to face my denial about money. I wanted money but I denied that want. I said things like, "I'm not a money person." As though I could attract what I was denying. I also didn't think of charging for my work because I didn't value myself enough to think I deserved an exchange for the value I was giving. For instance, I believe one of the reasons I was holding this book back was the possibility of making money off it. That possibility scared and maybe even shamed me, so that I always found good enough reasons not to finish the book when I should have.

If I were to update my relationship status with money on Facebook it would read: 'complicated'. I want it, I deny wanting it, I feel down when it doesn't come, and I attract just enough to keep me wanting more.

My therapist and I had a long talk about money one time and I was able to start coming to terms with my denial. It was also clear why I didn't value myself enough to put a money charge on my skills. Because of the inner conflicts I experienced, per societal expectations, I grew up thinking I wasn't enough. I also didn't think there was anything I could offer anyone that was of any value. When people told me I inspired them I always felt like a fraud. What was it about me that could possibly inspire anyone? Sometimes I thought they were patronizing me. I had accepted the lies that I was no good and that I had nothing to offer and the universe was giving me more of what I needed to feed that belief system. So I didn't have the courage to 'want' money in exchange for my commercially viable abilities.

I soon noticed that I would be happy when there was money in my account and sad when there wasn't any. The irony was I was more broke than not, therefore I was unhappy about money more than I was happy.

As I learned not to judge money as 'good' or 'bad', I learned I could be happy when I was broke just as I was happy when I was not broke. Happiness was a choice I could make every day, despite what my account balance said. So on the whole, money does not by itself make me happy. What money does is give me options, which is definitely a good thing.

I remember one time I went for a job interview and I was asked how much I'd like to be paid. I told them a figure and they were surprised because, as it would turn out, I had underestimated myself. I eventually got the job and a higher offer, and that was a learning curve. There was after all great value in what I was bringing to the table, and if other people could see it, why was I forcing myself to remain oblivious to it so that I could maintain a false notion that deep down didn't sit well with me?

As I started to see myself as worthy, I started changing my relationship with money. I no longer denied wanting money. I admitted it. I admit it.

I want money. I want lots of it. And I am deserving of it. This is my new truth about money.

9

LIES –
The Truth About Deception.

"Lying is a thriving vocation."

– Susanne Centlivre.

I found a simple definition of a lie online. It says, "Lying is saying something with the intent of creating a false belief or impression. It's an attempt to get someone to believe something that is not true." thehopeline.com

Cellphones have increased our ability to tell lies. *"Yes, I am on my way and will be there in 5 minutes,"* says the employee who overslept and only just jumped out of bed.

Gone are the days when parents told you to tell any visitor that showed up at the house that they weren't home. I was the kid that thought, "But you are around; why should I say you went out?" These innocent dealings were unconscious ways we learnt how to tell lies. "White lies," we call them.

I once told my mum I didn't hear when she called me, but of course this was a lie. I had only pretended to be asleep because I thought somebody wanted to ask me to get the remote control that was sitting just in front of her. But had I thought of it as a serious thing? No. After all, I had watched adults around me as they told 'white lies', 'harmless lies', and this was one of them.

We then grow up into people who lie to our parents, friends, siblings, strangers and even ourselves and then we have the nerve to be angry when a love interest tells us a lie. Do you see the double standards?

Have you ever wondered why you lie to strangers?

So you are out in a social gathering and you find yourself in the midst of four people whom you have never met before that day. Everyone is talking about travel plans and before you know it, you say, *"when I was in London five years ago…"* You proceed to spin a tale about the London trip that never happened. Why do you lie to people who you will never see again? What's the point?

All the times you have engaged in this business of telling lies, have you ever felt bad about it? Or did the little bad angel do a bad-angel dance because you had gotten away with the lie?

In trying to understand why people lie I had to look at my own life and the times that I told lies. What motivated those lies? I found that sometimes I lied just because I could get away with it. Other times, I lied to protect the people I cared about. And there were times when I felt there was no other option but to lie. Trouble came when I started lying to myself.

In relationships, I was always lying because I was never myself. I didn't feel good enough, smart enough, loveable enough or worthy of anyone's time. I let the men I dated treat me like trash because I didn't place any value on myself. In return I lied to them. I felt that lying was somehow repayment for the ways they treated me. If I couldn't get better treatment, then they wouldn't get honesty. I lied so much and most times for no reason, none at all.

When I did an online search about why people lied,

three reasons stood out for me. The first one was fear. People lie because they are afraid.

A child is afraid its parents might be upset over something so he lies. A boyfriend is worried his girl might misinterpret something he did so he lies. Friends are afraid to be upfront about their needs so they lie. At the point of telling a lie, no one is thinking about the consequences if the lies get found out because the current experience of fear is higher than the need for honesty.

Some lies can come from a place of innocence, in terms of feeling that one needs to protect the next person from pain. Some lies are calculated to get a pre-conceived result, and this brings us to another reason why people tell lies – to manipulate other human beings. For instance, a boyfriend knows the "right" lies to tell to get his girlfriend to do a certain thing a certain way. Friends are not exempt from these kinds of lies. A person who is close to you, who can tell what your reaction would be in a given situation, can manipulate you with lies in order to achieve sinister purposes.

As human beings, we try to interpret everything that happens in our lives. From wanting the new boss to perceive you a certain way, to wondering why the boyfriend is frowning, and maybe even wondering if the mother suspects something is off with your marriage, etc. We carry around these stories, thoughts, perception and fear of others and the world, and then we think lying is the only way to smoothen the roughness.

We tell one lie and get away with it. Then we tell another one. And another. We become LIARS.

Even though most people have lied at one point or another, and research even says we lie every day, the difference would be in the degree and frequency. There are some lies that have been told so many times by so many people that they have become a norm. An example is the rather common trend of people lying about their ages. They even have a term for it, “football age”, or “government age”. Some people have told this ‘age’ lie so often that they have even forgotten how old they really are. The origin of having fake ages often stems from the need to fit into a required age category for a job or sporting activity. It is manipulative and no matter how much glory one gets in the end, it is false and can come crashing like a pack of cards if the truth is ever unearthed.

Lies are a great disservice to interpersonal relationships but we human beings find it more difficult to be honest. There are a few times a lie has hurt my relationships with people, and whenever I find out I have been lied to, something in me reacts. I think, “How could I have been lied to? I’m smarter than this.” Ego, perhaps. But I have also been forced to hold a mirror up to myself.

In analyzing my reactions to lies in the past, I recognized that I had also told lies to people who

I caught lying to me. I see things like this from an energy perspective, which dictates that we often attract people, circumstances and events on the same vibrational level as ourselves. You therefore receive what you give. So whenever I didn't like what I was receiving, I had to check what I was giving. To change the circumstances around me, I had to change myself. I decided I would choose truth, and nothing but the truth, no matter how painful it would be. When I did this, I started being completely truthful with the people in my life, and I found that they could also be truthful with me too.

As we advance as human beings, needs and expectations continue to push us to tell lies, bigger lies than those we learned from childhood. No wonder the truth is in such short supply in our society. But we need to do better. We need to get mirrors, and we need to use them more often. This is the truth.

10

VALIDATION – Do You Approve of Me?

"Validate yourself first, and then you will receive the much-deserved healing validation from the rest of the world."

A. D. Posey.

My people-pleasing syndrome started long before I knew anything about people-pleasing. It was how I needed my mum to make me feel, it was expecting a boyfriend to tell me I was smart, it was hoping my friends really liked me and sometimes it was having a complete stranger post a comment like "wow" on my Facebook posts.

As a teenager, I thought I was getting something right if my mum approved of it. I sought her validation in every aspect of my life. Anytime I disappointed her, it felt as though I had disappointed the world. The thought of the embarrassment and shame I had caused made me coil into myself. I tried to do less of what she didn't like and more of what she liked, and hoped that I would finally get to a point where I made her happy and proud. But the more I did things to please her, the more it seemed like I failed to actually please her. I didn't understand this.

When I started dating, I was the same way. I had to please the object of my affection. If he wanted me to tell him the full details of my day with every person I spoke to and every person I texted, I would do it, not ever thinking of it as strange behavior. I permitted abnormal behavior because I was blinded by this need to please.

The first time a guy beat me I was seventeen years old. I didn't think it was strange. I thought he loved me too much and was only angry in that moment. And the other moments that followed. However, to call myself a victim would be half-truth because in retrospect, he was a victim too.

Whatever made him think it was okay to beat another human being, a "weaker" version of him according to society, had to be more than him being angry and therefore labeled an "abuser."

Unfortunately, we raise boys with the mentality that they are better than girls and this confuses a lot of them as grown men. They think they own the woman and most women are raised to think a man is the ultimate prize so they develop a need-to-please mentality around men. When these two meet there is bound to be a giving and receiving where the boy feels he is better than the girl and even owns her, while the girl feels worthy because the boy for instance tells her she is beautiful.

So the boyfriend in his early twenties and the teenage girlfriend, are both victims of a society that raised them wrongly in a world that is constantly changing.

I thought my boyfriend beating me was evidence of his love for me. I thought if only I could be better, if I could change, if I could understand when he was upset so that I kept quiet, if I could make him happy...

Oh, I wanted to make him happy. Never mind that I was not happy myself. I figured if he could be happy, that would somehow be enough for me.

People-pleasing showed up in my female friendships, too. In secondary school I had this friend I used to let have my personal stash of snacks and other ready-to-eat food items – 'provisions', as we called them, because I wanted her to like me enough to remain my friend. Come to think of it, she never had a lot of provisions herself, but she used to determine how we unwrapped and used mine. I wanted a friend, it didn't matter that she was eating my provisions. If it pleased her to finish them, as long as it made her happy, I had zero qualms.

In these days of the Internet, friendships have transcended the physical. We now have e-friends on social media. Sometimes, I think we make the mistake of thinking that a social media friend is a real friend. This is not to say that some true friendships have not been formed online, but I have found that in general, a Facebook friend is just that – a Facebook friend.

When I started seeking validation from Internet people, I thought it was normal. I would make a post and hope a particular person or set of persons would like it and perhaps make a comment. I also hoped they'd write what I considered a 'good comment.' I'd stay refreshing my Facebook phone-app regularly, to see if these people I cherished so much had rewarded my need for their 'likes' and comments. I just needed them to acknowledge me in some way.

It was exhausting.

I cannot put a finger on the exact day that I stopped

people-pleasing but I remember that making the transition from a full people pleaser to understanding that what people thought of me was none of my business, felt like a huge leap for me. Not just one of faith – believing that the right people would gravitate towards me nonetheless -- but also a leap that brought me joy, peace and happiness. What more could a girl ask for?

During my time in therapy, I learnt about personality disorders and mental health issues. When I started learning about co-dependency in particular, I looked at my own relationships and identified ways in which I might have been guilty. It turned out I was co-dependent in most of my relations, and in all of my intimate relationships.

People-pleasing was my way of trying to stay on everybody's good side. I felt I needed the people I cared about to validate me. I also felt I needed people who didn't know anything about me to validate me. I didn't know I could validate myself, that I could check my own boxes and live on my own terms.

It soon became too much for me – seeking external approval, crumbling when I didn't receive it, feeling elated when I did, and then aching for more where it came from. My sense of worth clearly lay in the hands of other people, but at the end of the day none of that really mattered. The crowd that applauded me one day could easily disapprove of me the next day because I wasn't feeding into the image it had of me. How much of that could I really take? How much expanding and shrinking on the terms of other people could I experience before finally being worn out by the exertion of it all? It was emotionally and mentally unhealthy for me, and I just could not go on being that way. I was done. Just done.

Seeking validation from others is like something hanging around your neck. It weighs you down and stops you from moving as quickly as you would like. What you don't realize is that you can easily take it off when you realize you don't need it. I took it off when I got tired enough.

I now live a life that's worthy of me - a life by me, and for me; applauding myself when I need to, and being wholly content in my own validation of myself.

11

TRANSITION –
The Pain Of Change.

"Life is pleasant. Death is peaceful. It's the transition that's troublesome."

Isaac Asimov.

A change of perception leads to a change of mind, which leads to a change in your inner state. Here's what I mean. When I started asking real questions around god, religion, faith, belief, church and spirituality, I had to first accept where my head was. I had to accept that I didn't believe most of the things I had claimed to believe my whole life. After having absorbed all the things I had grown up hearing in church, I had allowed myself to be forcefully convinced of things that I was now feeling very different about.

I was at a point where I was realizing that I could believe what I wanted to personally believe. I could make my own way by examining all that was available to be examined, and coming to my own conclusions. This new way of seeing things came with a lot of anger. I was angry with the people who had tried to convince me of these things in church, I was angry with my parents who introduced me to that life in the first place. I was angry with myself for lying to myself that I believed in all of that, when all the time, I really did not. After the anger, I made peace with it. I accepted that I was an 'unbeliever', and I started asking myself what I really believed.

When I figured out what I believed, I naturally had a change in perception, which led to a change of mind and a change in my inner state. When I stopped going to church, I gave out all my Bibles and Christian literature, and I started feeling peaceful because I was finally living my truth about my real beliefs.

My biggest transition was in religion. I went from believing to doubting and then total unbelief. I got a lot of strong reactions at every stage of the change I was experiencing. This was expected, as most times transition comes with a lot of pain. The pain of losing the people who once supported you, the pain of leaving behind the things you had previously believed with your life, the pain of starting afresh, choosing again, admitting that you didn't quite 'know'.

There is also the pain of seeming confused to yourself and others, and this for me was the deepest pain in my transition. One day I was proclaiming one thing and another day I was denying everything I had once defended with my entire being.

When you change your perception, you see differently. The situations and people remain the same, but you see them with new eyes. This turn-around will affect some humans in your life. Some of them will not like the new you, others will find you befuddling, and will begin to tell different stories about why they think you are how you are. Whatever explanations they peddle, will be for their own peace of mind, because what they will be dealing with, is a change in your inner state, something you have little control over.

People notice the change in your inner state because most times it is a complete one-eighty degree turn from what you were once about. In my case, I went from being a tongue-speaking believer to a non-believer. *"It has to be the end times,"* many argued.

It took me a while to accept my unbelief, and even after I did, I had to face backlash from friends, family and foes while in pursuit of my truth. It hurt to be ostracized, judged, condemned and left to 'die', but in the end it was all worth it.

I learned that the pain of change is a necessary right of passage in growth and evolving. I own every bit of my journey and I appreciate my transition periods. They were all interesting times.

12

RELIGION – My Journey To Unbelief.

"Religion is the impotence of the human mind to deal with occurrences it cannot understand."

Karl Max.

My first religious/church experience had me in a white gown from my head to my toes, complete with a cap. I remember I had to take off my little slippers before going into the church building. During one of those services, my slippers were stolen and I had to walk home barefoot. This is all the memory I have of my church-experience as a child.

A few years later, when we moved to Abuja, I attended a different kind of church. This time I wore colorful dresses with shoes to match. What I liked most was that I didn't need to remove my shoes before entering the building. Asides this little detail, I don't remember much of that experience either.

In university, I had no interest in attending church. The good news was nobody could make me attend, so Sundays were an extension of Saturdays. I slept longer and it was peaceful, as most people had gone to church. During the five years I spent in university, I had countless invitations to attend church for a 'life-changing experience.'

First of, I didn't want to change my life; it was going just great. Secondly, the way these inviters tried to convince you to come to their church reminded me of sales people. Everyone was trying to prove that his or her god was the true god.

In my final year, I finally joined a church. The reason was my fear of failing and repeating a semester while my mates proceeded to law school. I was determined to meet this god and beg him to help me pass my exams. I even promised to serve him for the rest of my life if I somehow did well and got admitted to law school with my mates.

I passed.

I was miraculously proceeding to law school with my mates. Surely it was god and I felt obliged to keep my promise. It's clear to me now that I created a god based on the transactional manner in which human beings tend to treat each other. 'Scratch my back and I scratch yours'.

I also decided to subject my life to an illusion that my actions were judged, and that they determined whether god would be kind or wicked to me.

By the time I graduated from law school, I figured it was time to fulfill my promise of serving this god that had helped me come this far. Every church I attended, I was committed to 'working' for god, one way or another. If I wasn't giving money for projects, I was sacrificing my Saturdays to clean the church, or working as an usher, stewardess, etc. In my mind, the more I committed my time to church activities, the more I pleased this god and this could mean the difference between going to hell or heaven.

After a while, I noticed that the people in church who claimed to serve god were after their own interests. Some people were living double lives. They would have one face in church, and a different face outside church. I too, found myself living that lie. I was 'Sister Ese' in church and after church, I was, well, Ese. I wanted to be the same person in and out of church but it was impossible because the church wouldn't have accepted the real Ese.

I once had an opportunity to ask a church leader how he managed to live a double life without feeling bad about it and he said something along the lines of "god doesn't necessarily mind what you do or don't do." This statement changed my whole perception of the church and religion. Over time, I began to see how these 'leaders' controlled members to the point where members started thinking of them as gods. I call them 'god of men'.

I passed through that phase of seeing a leader as a god. I started to go through the motions of church activity. I ignored what seemed wrong, and focused on pleasing this god who helped me pass my final exams in school, as well as venerating the gods of men, who seemed to be the leaders of the cause.

As a teenager, I heard about the 'holy ghost' and how to receive his gift of speaking in other tongues. I think it was the ability to speak a different language that interested me. The pastors prayed for everyone that came out to receive the holy ghost, with evidence of it being the 'speaking in tongues'. Of all the teenagers that stood up, I was the only one who didn't speak this new language despite constant nudging that all I had to do was open my mouth and 'let it flow'.

I opened my mouth wide. I considered speaking gibberish just so I could fit in with the rest of the teenagers who had received the gift but I didn't want to pretend like I got something I didn't. I left church that day believing the holy spirit didn't like me. Why else would he give everyone else his gifts except me? I felt sad. The pastor assured me that I would speak in tongues later that night at home. He said some people don't get to 'speak' immediately but it didn't mean that they didn't receive the gift. So, I was not to worry; I would be able to speak it eventually. That night at home, I couldn't sleep; I practiced speaking in tongues until I got into the flow of it. I couldn't wait for the next Sunday to tell the pastor I spoke in tongues after all.

The year two thousand was when I started asking real questions about the belief I had claimed my entire life. I always wondered about god. I thought about heaven and hell a lot, too. I worried if I was doing enough to please god and if it all meant something at the end of the day. I think I always had my doubts about the Christian god and his/her motives with humanity but I never had the guts to follow my doubts where they wanted to lead. The more I asked questions, the more I was told about faith and belief. Someone told me that I needed to believe and not doubt but somewhere in my mind I knew my questions were valid, I just didn't have the confidence to ask them for too long but they stayed in my mind.

My reasoning started with, "why would god chose to save me over the girl on the other side of the planet?" I'd always see stories of wars and suffering in the news and I wasn't feeling so lucky anymore. I believed when I was told that god cared about me and was providing for me but seeing as I prayed for the people who were suffering I wondered why god didn't care enough to help them too. One day I asked the ultimate question, *"what if this god narrative is a lie?"*

That question scared me so I didn't listen for any responses that might come from the voices in my head. I needed my entire belief-system to be true. I wasn't sure I could handle the fact that I might have been living and believing a lie. However, when I was ready or should I say desperate enough, I started thinking about religion from an objective place.

From birth a person is told what to believe and thrown into these religious institutions for reinforcement. By the time a child goes through the formative stage of their development, they have already formed beliefs around another person's idea of life and death.

A primary school in Lagos had children singing praise-songs every morning. I could hear the children during assembly screaming at the top of their lungs. They were told to pray and sing praises to god for about thirty minutes. Every. Morning. That to me was programming. Those children didn't have a choice and they believed that god was listening to them sing and pray.

And this is how beliefs are formed. Most of the things people call beliefs are ideas that have been programmed in them before they had a choice. These ideas form the core of who they think they are to the point that they fight anything that opposes these ideas, which they have adopted as beliefs.

One Sunday morning, I sat in church as the preacher was preaching and I asked myself questions about belief. I would later find the jotter I was writing down my thoughts in and remember how disconnected I was from the service that morning.

The note is dated 07.04.13 and it reads:

WHAT DO YOU BELIEVE?

What does it mean to believe?

Do you really believe what you claim to believe?

Are you lying to yourself and your mind about what you have claimed to believe?

Definition: To trust and be confident in… fully persuaded by…

Can you confidently say you believe in god?

Do you know god for yourself? Are you stuck in religion?

Are you still claiming to believe because to say otherwise will make you a liar?

Nothing happens without you first truly believing. As long as you continue denying what you believe or claiming to believe what you don't, you will be stuck. Don't be stuck in religion. Nothing is about to happen, stop constantly waiting on something. All that is going to happen has already happened, get your ass out of waiting mode and get in the flow.

There is no success without a prize. Success must cost you something. If you hope to get where you are going doing the same things you have always done, going in the same circle, fighting the same demons, then you are lying to yourself.

It starts with what you believe. It starts with getting all the crap you have learnt out of your mind. It starts with being honest with yourself about where you are and about what stops you from getting where you need to go.

Why aren't you confident about what you believe?

When I wrote this note, I thought I was asking the people in church who were responding to the preacher's message. I know now that I was writing it for myself. I was asking myself if I really believed because I had already begun to seriously doubt everything.

I began to conclude that religion was dangerous, as most of us in my church saw our pastor as a demigod. It was he who heard from god and gave us instructions. The danger with that for me was, what if he wasn't hearing from god and was just controlling people for the heck of it and his congregation of religious people were simply submitting themselves to be used and controlled?

How else do you explain a parent subjecting their child to torture or death because some spiritual leader claims said child is a witch? How do we explain people strapping on bombs to kill themselves and others because of promises of a better afterlife and sex with virgins? Why are religious people the most judgmental people in any setting? If you do not believe what they believe, you are branded an enemy, an unbeliever, and one not worthy of their friendship.

I decided I wanted to know this god for myself or abandon religion completely. I bought all the versions of the Bible I could find; I also bought a Bible dictionary, Bible commentaries and a Bible encyclopedia. I was convinced that somewhere in those books were the answers I sought. I read the Bible every day and it was such a chore. I attended church services and after every service, I'd go back to read what was taught and find where in my life I was meeting up or falling short.

As a church-worker, I was close to the pastors and one time I had an affair with a pastor. I couldn't get over the guilt for a long time. First I wondered why it was easy for me to fall for whatever the pastor was telling me. I considered myself smart enough to smell bullshit because I wasn't a child. I also thought that if the pastor could stoop so low as to have an affair with me, then maybe god didn't care all that much about the things we said god cared about.

I asked the pastor a few questions about the implication of our affair but what I heard was something about a level of grace available to me that I wasn't aware of. The pastor decided he was going to teach me about that grace but something in me thought it was better not to know the grace than know it and live a double life forever.

For a long time, I carried the guilt of having an affair with a pastor like a wet blanket. I thought leaving the church and burying what happened was going to save me but it didn't. Instead I was suffering inside. I couldn't tell my family because I feared they would not believe me and would maybe judge me. I also couldn't tell my friends because I didn't want anyone laughing at me or spreading gossip about me.

I eventually told a friend and his reaction and questions told me I had made a big mistake by confiding in him. As the weeks went by, other mutual friends heard about my affair with the pastor. I left the church, cut myself off from those friends, and started attending another church altogether. My hope was that I would rebuild myself into somebody who was worthy of being on earth, but the guilt followed me everywhere I went. It became too heavy for me to bear, and I eventually had to tell other pastors who I thought could help me.

This worsened my situation because I was 'suspected' for blackmail and 'seduction of a man of god.' The nightmares started and sometimes I couldn't wait for the day to be over even though I didn't like the nights. It felt like my life was going in the wrong direction.

Tired of all the judgment, I then decided to write a post about the affair and free myself of whatever power the secret had over me. The day I published the post was the beginning of my understanding of this religion I practiced and what I claimed to believe. People from around the country were writing all sorts of things about me. Suddenly, I was a person of interest and every time I went online I was bullied. I wondered why people were so quick to judge and cuss at me for something they knew nothing about. However, I experienced peace, and the nightmares stopped. I felt free. It no longer mattered what anyone thought about me.

What mattered to me then was to learn what god thought about it and then focus on being a better human. I learnt that a lot of pastors do what they like and the members are the first to defend them. I learnt that my emotional dependence and the natural human need for connection made me reach out to a gathering of people I thought could help me grow a spine. With zero confidence and no faith in myself, it was easy to look up to people who seemed confident to help me determine my path in life. After the affair, I was better able to see my reality without the colored glasses. My doubt in all things religion returned full force and I was sure I didn't buy the god narrative.

The first thing I did was cut out prayer from my

routine. After a year of no prayer, no church and no Bible reading, I gave out all my Bibles, Bible dictionary and every Christian literature on my bookshelf. I was ready to stop living in denial and face my reality. What happened next was confirmation that I was on the right path. I started meeting people who doubted what they claimed to believe. I also met people who were scared to go where the doubt was leading. I could relate with that and I began to feel an obligation to help people like that go where their hearts were leading them.

There were Christians who felt it was their duty to win me back to god and there were others who felt it was in their place to pronounce my doom. All of these reminded me of the time I blogged about my affair and Christians all over the place were condemning me. Initially, I would engage them and cuss them out but after a few weeks I felt that engaging them was a needless pursuit. I focused instead on the new path I was on. I was awakening to something bigger than me and the people who attacked me paled in comparison to the new truths I was experiencing.

One day, I declared my unbelief and called myself an unbeliever. That was the last time I pretended to believe what I didn't believe. Till date, I don't engage in religious arguments but I talk about consciousness and awakening every chance I get. I don't hate Christians or religious people in general. I don't even hate the pastor I had an affair with. I see him now as my biggest teacher on religious matters.

If what happened had never happened, I wouldn't have gotten the push I needed to explore my beliefs. I would have been living a lie to this day, claiming to believe what I didn't. Today I feel free. I am free to pursue my beliefs if any, I am free to explore my consciousness, I am free to love all people because I do not have a bias based on religious affiliations. I am also free to attend church or any religious gathering of my choice, if I so please. Despite the human factor that has polluted religion, I know that every aspect of learning is valuable and I wouldn't judge any part of it.

Today I can declare that I am Ese and my religion is LOVE.

13

GUILT AND SHAME – My Public Breakdown.

"Guilt and its handmaiden, shame, can paralyze us, or catalyze us into action. Appropriate guilt can function as social glue, spurring one to make reparations for wrongs. Excessive rumination about one's failures, however, is a surefire recipe for resentment and depressing thoughts"

Psychology Today.

Guilt and shame are very alike but significantly different. The same action may give rise to both guilt and shame, where guilt reflects how we feel about ourselves and shame reflects our knowing that our actions have injured someone else. For example, when I published the blog about my experience with the pastor, I felt guilt on one hand and shame on the other. I was guilty as charged. After all, I was an adult, how could I have been so stupid? I also felt shame because I knew my actions caused my family a lot of pain. My guilt and shame experience was on such a massive scale that I thought it would kill me. Every day, I woke up asking what I was going to hear or see next.

I wasn't at home at the time so I was spared any judgment that might have come from family. I also didn't have a lot of friends around me either. I wasn't sure what my friends thought or felt so I kept away. Only two people were aware of my whereabouts. I was in a hotel somewhere in Abuja hiding away from the rest of the world. Everyday my best friend, Ezinne would come stay with me. She would sometimes go online to read what people were saying. She never read anything out to me though, except it was a funny comment. She would remind me who I was and make me stay focused on why I blogged about the experience.

I didn't see my family during the blog episode because I knew I had caused massive shame and I didn't want to face what it meant to them. I also feared going out because I grew up in Abuja, and since my pictures were all over the place, it was easy to identify me. I feared that some religious people might have attacked me and perhaps even set me on fire, and from the kinds of emails I was getting, I was right to think so.

After a couple of weeks living in hiding, I decided it was time to heal from my guilt and shame. I did an online search on "how to overcome guilt and shame."

The first thing that caught my eye was a TED Talk by Brene Brown on "The power of vulnerability." She introduced herself as a 'shame researcher', and I knew I had found the person I needed to hear from. After watching that talk, nothing changed inside me but I enjoyed it so much I wanted more. I searched for her and found more talks, interviews and books on shame, guilt, vulnerability, worthiness and resilience. I felt I had found someone who could talk me through my shame and guilt. My friend was doing good but she was trying to help me avoid the pain that came with the shame and guilt, while Brene Brown was telling me it was okay, even normal, to feel those things. It was part of the process.

I started learning a lot about shame, and how to develop empathy for myself, how to surround myself with people I could share my shame stories with. Brene says anytime someone is using something you shared with him or her about you against you, they are trying to hurt you. In my case, I had friends who used the blog story to shame me. Some friends walked away from me, some stayed to see how long I could keep up, and some old friends showed up. Strangers also showed up, and every day I wondered when it would all end.

A few months after the blog story broke I thought I was ready to read what people had been saying about me. I did a Google search of my name, and the things I saw almost sent me into a depressive state. I wanted to explain to everybody that I wasn't the kind of person they thought I was. I wanted to defend why I published the post. I wanted to say I didn't mean to hurt anybody, and that I hadn't been thinking about anybody at the time I published the post. I thought about myself and the nightmares I had to endure, I wondered when it would all end, I thought about connecting with one other human who had experienced the same thing I had experienced at my church, just to be able to show them that they weren't alone. But all of that didn't seem to matter. I was the devil and these people were condemning me to hell.

On the flip side, there were people who reached out to me to tell me they believed me and I was going to be all right. Even though I liked what they were saying, I wasn't really hearing them. I was consumed by my own self-loathing and constantly wished that it had all been a dream I would someday wake up from. I also got emails from people who were living in guilt and shame because of their own choices.

A few ladies shared stories of affairs they had with their pastors. One of them was a teenager who said her mother took all the children to be deflowered by their pastor. She said she knew something was wrong with that experience but she had never been able to share her story because she was afraid and confused.

Something about these stories renewed my strength. They didn't make me feel bold or courageous as one might have thought, but I felt justified that my 'shame story' somehow reached the people who needed to hear it. I knew I couldn't help anyone because I didn't know how to, but I was happy they could share their stories with me and, and I hope that this gave them the kind of peace I had myself gotten by blogging about mine.

In May 2015, I found myself testifying at an event, about how I had experienced guilt and shame and it didn't kill me, but made me stronger. As I spoke those words, there was no shame at all. Instead, I felt empowered. If I hadn't experienced guilt and shame on a large scale, I would not have understood guilt and shame like I did at that event, and like I do now.

Brene Brown taught me to develop empathy for myself and understand shame to the point that it didn't disempower me. I learnt that and today I live shame free. This doesn't mean I don't feel shame at all on some days. It just means that shame does not cripple me. I have enough light to shine on shame so it doesn't stay with me longer than it needs to.

As for guilt, I find that it is a needless emotion. When there is guilt, I usually talk to the person or people involved just to clear the air. I don't deny any part of it. I accept it fully as part of my life's experiences. I know that everything that happens in my life serves a purpose and I am open to all the lessons my experiences bring.

"The shame story I was so afraid of turned out to be the greatest gift of my life because it released me." Ese.

14

THERAPY –

Am I Crazy?

"Writing is a form of therapy; sometimes I wonder how all those who do not write, compose, or paint can manage to escape the madness, melancholia, the panic and fear which is inherent in a human situation."

— Graham Greene, Ways Of Escape

In August 2013, I got a lot of requests for interviews; radio stations, television, blogs and newspapers emailed me to discuss my blog post, which was now famous or infamous depending on perspective. I felt as though the reason for publishing the post was going to be lost if I was talking to everyone about it so I declined all the requests with a follow up blog post titled "Going Forward."

In this post I addressed the various interview seekers once and for all, telling them that I didn't plan to grant any interviews. I also decided to stop talking about the pastor altogether. I then assumed that things were going to return to normal since I had decided to move forward, but I couldn't have been further from reality. It seemed a lot of people became interested in my personal life at that point.

How could a single, Nigerian girl write about sex with a married pastor? The nerve! There were of course some people who believed my story, but many were convinced I had told lies, and then others sat on the fence, popcorn in hand, waiting for events to unfold.

Everything I wrote on my blog was judged through the lenses of that initial post so writing became a pain in the ass. I was frustrated. I thought I was losing my mind. I knew I brought it on myself but I needed everyone to just let me be.

I started getting paid offers to write and I accepted one of them. It was a newspaper and they were not going to force me to write about anything I wasn't comfortable with. I was free to write about whatever I wanted but there was a catch that didn't quite work for me. The deal then went bad and I ignored the fact that I had suddenly become a person of interest. I tweeted about my experience.

A few hours after my tweets, I heard that the same tweets had appeared on the blog of the number one blogger in Nigeria. All other blogs did the usual copy and paste and things escalated.

News of the tweets reached my mother and she was unhappy that once again, I was in the news. I was bringing shame to her and my entire family. We had a long talk that night. She reminded me to think about my siblings and parents when I wrote. She also opined that there was something wrong with my actions and asked if I'd like to see a therapist for evaluation.

Everything in me wanted to refuse and fight the idea of talking to some stranger about things even I didn't fully understand. I wanted to say no, but I said yes. There was no fighting left in me, so I agreed to see the therapist.

When we got to the therapist's office, I was cold. She asked my mum what the problem was and my mum told her a couple of things she noticed in me growing up. Most of what she said centered around my inability to do things in ways that were generally acceptable. She said I had a normal birth and childhood, but that as I grew up, I seemed to deviate from the straight and narrow. She said I couldn't hold down a job or relationship. She didn't fail to add that I was past marriageable age and even though I had gotten a few proposals, I didn't want to 'settle down.' When she was done, the therapist thanked her for sharing all she did and asked me if I had anything to say.

"No!" was my sharp response.

There was no way I was going to talk about anything to a stranger especially in the presence of my mum. My mum was too far removed from my reality. I remembered that time she took me to Los Angeles. She said she wanted us to have a daughter-mother time so we could talk about everything I wanted to do and what was going on with me. I opened up to her that I didn't want to be a lawyer because I was scared I didn't know anything about law and was afraid to go into the world of litigation. She asked what I wanted to do and the best I could come up with was, 'teach.' I said I wanted to be a teacher.

"Teacher?" she asked, surprised.

I said yes. I didn't know what I wanted to teach though. I couldn't figure out what I knew for sure, let alone how to teach it to someone else, but it felt natural to want to do it anyway.

Mother said nothing. I would later find out that she

took this story to my sibling and questioned my ideas. This broke trust on a level that was unredeemable. So no, I wasn't talking to or around my mum about my thoughts and feelings.

The therapist asked my mum to give us some time to talk alone, after which my mum was going to come in to talk to her alone, and then we would have a group talk and decide how to move forward.

I thought that was going to be the end of therapy. A day of talking, probably a group hug in the end, and all would be well.

As soon as my mum shut the door behind her, the therapist looked at me with a smile.

"Do you want to be here?" she asked.

"I'm not sure what you mean. I'm here, no?" I responded.

She went on to say that therapy is expensive and she didn't like to take people's monies if there would be no commitment from the patient to follow through on the sessions and exercises that would come up during the course of therapy.

She asked again if I wanted to be there. She said it was important I was there for myself and not for my mum. *"It will be a waste of your time and mine if you aren't here because you want to be."* She concluded.

After some consideration, I decided I wanted to be there. I told her I hadn't wanted to come initially because I thought seeing a therapist meant I was crazy and I knew I wasn't crazy. She said if I were crazy, I'd need a psychiatrist. And that we would start off by evaluating me to determine what I needed exactly.

We talked for about half an hour. I enjoyed talking to her because she didn't make me feel judged. She was soft-spoken and sounded like she truly wanted to help me, and I could use someone like her on my team, especially after many friends had cut me off that same year. I had caused them unbearable shame and I wasn't worth the friendship. We finished the session and planned the evaluation for the next week.

Come evaluation day I was put in a room to answer tons of questions. I initially thought it was a stupid exercise, but I answered all the questions as honestly and as quickly as I could. When I was done, she said she would get back to me with my results and what was needed to commence therapy. She handed me a cup to pee in. She needed to test for drugs.

On the day we met to analyze my results and discuss plans for sessions, she talked a little about mental health disorders and the different clusters. I was diagnosed with "borderline personality disorder." Until that moment, I'd never heard of it. I made a mental note of it so I could read about it.

The drug tests came back negative. Then she said we were going to see three times a week for a couple of months until there was improvement in behavioral patterns.

And so it began.

Therapy was the highlight of my weeks. I enjoyed talking to her as we explored my childhood memories and experiences. I also enjoyed trying out the exercises and observing my responses to everyday challenges. I was beginning to see a bigger picture and the possibility of moving forward in creating the kind of life I wanted. I was also interested in doing for others what she was doing for me. This was the reason I started courses in Counseling and Child Psychology.

After a few months in therapy, I started seeing how I was my own biggest problem. Because I had always kept journals, I was able to go back to read my writings through the years and I started seeing a pattern.

I always wrote about abuse, pain, hurt, fear, and my inability to move forward. It seemed like every time I took one step forward, I took two steps back. But there I was, finally starting to make some sense of my life after three decades of my existence. It was as though prior to that time I had been sleepwalking through life, unaware how one event connected to another and how they all came together to form this big bowl of hot mess.

I decided to help myself along with the great job my therapist was doing. I started reading all I could find on self-help, motivation, healing, recovery, and anything that was going to move me forward into the new life I envisioned for myself.

I learnt things like, "co-dependency," "learned helplessness," "Stockholm syndrome," and the importance of self-love.

I became a committed listener/follower of Iyanla Vanzant, Oprah Winfrey, Eckhart Tolle, Tony Robbins, Marie Forleo, Daniella LaPorte, Marianne Williamson, Otiti Jasmine (this is my friend who endured years of PTSD and she was very generous in sharing her experiences with me), and a few others.

Something Iyanla Vanzant said in a YouTube video I watched rang true to me and never left my mind. She said, *"people do what they do based on who they are and the information they have at the time."*

I thought about this a lot and realized it was true not just in my life, but in the lives of the people closest to me as well. My mum, dad, friends, lovers, and even colleagues did all they did based on who they were, and the information they had at the time. I also did all I did based on who I was and the information available to me at the time. It was time to forgive the others and myself. It was time to move forward.

It seemed I had gotten my act together. Until I got married and old demons popped up. During this time, I had stopped therapy because I thought I had gotten all I needed to live a normal life. I didn't know at the time that certain things lay dormant in us until a person or event awakened them. In my case, the person was my husband and the event was being married and sharing space with him.

15

LOVE AND MARRIAGE – I Didn't Marry For Love.

"If you don't love yourself, you can't love others. You won't be able to love others. If you have no compassion for yourself then you are not capable of developing compassion for others."

Dalai Lama.

A few months after therapy, I felt I was ready to get my life together and marriage seemed like the best place to start. I thought getting married was going to prove I had sorted my life out.

The decision to marry was a quick one. I found that it made my family happy. I wasn't sure if they were happy I was getting my life sorted out, or that I was finally going to be somebody else's problem. They were happy and that made me happy. Or so I thought.

As we prepared for the wedding ceremony, I had a lot of thoughts around not being ready. I knew in my heart that I didn't want to be married but with all the good vibes I was getting I figured marriage couldn't be all that hard. So, I jumped in.

A few months after the wedding, I started wondering why I got married. I didn't trust my husband so I was always suspicious of everything he did. This lack of trust had something to do with how we met and a lot to do with my general distrust for men. Then, I found out I was pregnant. I was going to be a mummy. This didn't bring the kind of joy I expected as per what I saw in the movies, and that sort of felt strange.

As my belle grew, my husband and I grew apart. I couldn't stand being with him, I wanted to get away. I wanted to end the marriage and focus on single-motherhood. I thought I had made a mistake marrying him and I was determined to correct that mistake.

When I was five months pregnant, I left the country. I didn't leave because I wanted to have my baby abroad; I left because I couldn't stand to be around my husband. And I believed he couldn't stand to be around me either.

While away, I was lonely every day. I wanted to come back to Nigeria but I couldn't imagine sharing space with my husband. I thought I was better off being alone by myself in a faraway country than being lonely while living in the same house with him. Seeing as I was going to be there a while I decided I was going to make the best of my time.

Instead of brooding over a marriage I thought was over, I decided to start learning how to live alone. I also started reading books about single mothers. One of the first books I bought was titled, "Single mothers raising sons in a fatherless home" by Dr. William James. I knew some single mothers complained about how difficult it was raising kids alone so I wanted to prepare myself before my son arrived earth side. I also stopped wearing my wedding band. I thought it was time to get used to not being married before I left the marriage. I also felt lost as a person so I decided I couldn't give birth to someone else until I had given birth to myself. I knew I needed to find some form of peace and acceptance of my situation and myself.

I started yoga and swimming aerobics at the neighborhood gym, I also met new people every other day. I took long walks, made videos of my walks, sang at the top of my lungs at night, and ate everything I could find. I stopped calling my husband and he wasn't calling me much either. I was learning to live with the 'pain of my mistake' of marrying him. Many nights I was lonely but didn't feel alone anymore. I started keeping a 'Dear Kendrick' journal where I recorded all the ways I was feeling with regards my pregnancy.

When I was eight months pregnant, my friends organized a baby shower for me. I was truly happy that day. I danced the night away and received tons of presents. That night back home I wrote in my journal about how happy I was. I spoke to Kendrick, my unborn child, and assured him we were going to do just fine.

My husband called me a few times that day and I acted like I was cool with him. He was expecting his visa to travel for the birth of our son and I secretly wished he would not get it. However, he got the visa. He was going to come be with me and, funnily, I was excited at the thought. I tried to fight this excitement and considered telling the midwives I didn't want him in the labor room. I was going to 'show him', for making me feel so miserable during the time I lived with him right after marriage.

He arrived on New Year's Eve. For someone who was so upset at the man, I was at the airport to welcome him. Everybody thought I was too heavy to make the airport trip. They wanted me to wait for him to get to the house but I wasn't hearing it. I dressed up warm and took a jacket and hand gloves for him. When I saw him at the airport, I jumped on him with my big belly. I felt happy.

We hung out that night watching fireworks. I didn't remember how upset I was. Or maybe I just buried it deep down until it was ready to rear its head again. We didn't go back to the house that night. We stayed at some hotel we had booked for his visa application and therefore couldn't cancel without a fine.

The next day we had breakfast, talked and went back home to be with the rest of the family. We went out every day until Kendrick arrived on the 9th of January. I couldn't sort out my emotions around how I felt concerning his arrival but I stuck with some form of happy. The day we circumcised Kendrick was the same day hubby left for Nigeria. Then Kendrick and I remained about two weeks before coming back to Nigeria to join his father.

The day we arrived, I started feeling those feelings of resentment again. I remembered the stuff that made me travel when I was five months pregnant. I remembered all the times I tried to talk to him and was met with a cold wall. I remembered feeling lonely while living with him. Now I had my baby, I had company. I didn't need his company anymore. I was ready to leave him properly and finally, but I couldn't leave at the time. Kendrick was still very 'new'. So I stayed, and started planning my exit.

Almost a year later, I decided to leave him. Nothing anyone said could change my mind. I thought I was better off by myself and it seemed that way for a while. After a few months we decided to actively make things work. We went for couple's therapy.

During couple's therapy, we talked about a lot. The kinds of things that came up for me went back to before we got married. At some point during one session, I had to allow him privacy with the mind therapist as she felt he was a bit guarded because of me. When I returned, he had been crying. By the end of our session, I was beginning to think differently about my decision to end our marriage. It was clear to me that I had been judging him and couldn't see anything good about him. I had felt he was wrong for me, and I had made a mistake marrying him. I had concluded that to make things right we needed to be apart from each other. He on the other hand, felt we could work things out.

I had to do a lot of soul-searching and ask a lot of questions around where my fears came from. I learnt that I had trust issues even before I met him. It wasn't about what he did or didn't do. It was about my mind and the fact that it had already been made up about men in general, even before I met or married him.

As I started working through my own issues, I started seeing him for who he was. I started listening to him and actually hearing him, and I was finally willing to give our marriage a second chance.

It was in this time I started learning about true love. In his book, "The Breakthrough Experience," John Dermartini talks about the duality of life. In relationships, especially marriage, he says it's an illusion to expect only happiness and bliss. According to him, we oscillate between happy and sad, highs and lows, negatives and positives. He says this is how it is with life in general. There are always two sides happening in life at every point, and to expect only one side is illusionary. This helped me understand why I was having such a hard time in my marriage. I thought I was meant to be happy throughout my marriage to my hubby, therefore anytime we had disagreements I was confused and thought something was wrong.

I became conscious of this duality in my marriage. I also started getting comfortable with conflict. In the past, I would avoid conflict so peace could reign but I learnt that sometimes there would be peace, and other times there could be war. It was up to me to relinquish judgment and allow everything pan out as it should.

My husband is not violent so I never had cause to fear for my life. Once I made peace with this duality in my relationship with him (and by extension my entire life), I felt grounded. I was able to pursue my dreams outside him and I didn't have any unreasonable expectations of him. I also didn't need him to feed my insecurities. I decided to accept myself fully and, by accepting myself, I was finally able to accept him.

I love my husband. I can say that now. And I'm not talking about the kind of love that changes like the weather. I love him because I love him and I am committed to our marriage and to him. I know we will have ups and downs but instead of planning to run, I understand these are normal experiences in life and all is as it should be. It has always been.

16

MOTHERHOOD – Postpartum Blues, Postpartum Body and Postpartum Sex.

"Birth is the epicenter of women's power."

Ani Difranco.

I walked into the bathroom on the morning of January 7th 2015 and, as I took my panties off, my water broke. I forgot all I had been taught at antenatal class. I sat on the toilet bowl to pee and was expecting painful contractions to follow but nothing happened. After peeing I went into the room and informed hubby my waters broke.

A few hours later, we were at the hospital where I was taken to a room for examination. The midwife said there were no signs my waters broke. She said the water was meant to keep coming out and it wouldn't just happen once and stop. She told me to go back home and stay alert for more water coming out and possible contractions.

When we got home I was in the room waiting to feel something, but nothing happened. I didn't go out that day but stayed home, ready to go to the hospital whenever baby was ready. I did a search about water breaking without contractions, as I was sure my waters broke that morning. I read something about fore and hind waters and that put my mind at ease.

Two days later my son arrived earth side and I wasn't as happy as I thought I'd be. I figured it was because I was tired, and I believed I was going to snap out of it soon. When we got back home I was happier than in the hospital but I was still very doubtful I could be a mummy. I needed help with everything. I read a lot on What To Expect forum. Sometimes I was plain paranoid; checking on my sleeping baby and wondering if he had stopped breathing. Information overload about SIDS (Sudden Infant Death Syndrome) made me very fearful.

I had challenges breastfeeding initially and that didn't help the way I felt about this new life I had brought into the world. I didn't feel confident that I was enough for him. I was always goggling something or calling my mum several times a day to ask the same question over and over again. It seemed like he was always breastfeeding, so I started calling him Boobman.

At night Boobman would wake up to feed and I would think about kicking my hubby in the head for not even getting up with me to offer a backrub or his company. Sometimes he'd put the pillow over his head as though Boobman's cry was disturbing him, and I would sit there wondering if I would ever want to have another baby.

I sank deeper into the blues. I knew I wasn't happy but it didn't make sense that I wasn't happy especially as I just had a baby. And even though I had heard a little about postpartum depression, I was in complete denial. I didn't think it was possible that I was depressed. I was supposed to be happy so I acted happy as much as I could. Inside my head was where the real battle happened. I also didn't like my changing body and this dislike was reinforced every time someone told me I was fat.

This self-loathing started eating into my relationship

with everyone around me, especially my husband. I was eating more than usual, mostly for comfort. I convinced myself I didn't care what anyone thought about my body so I was going to prove I didn't care by eating all I could find. I'd wake up by 2am for some bread, I'd have chocolates and biscuits by the bed. I was always binging on soda.

As my body changed, I stopped looking at it in the mirror. I would walk into the shower with my towel on so I don't see my body in the mirror. Nobody knew what I was experiencing because I was very hostile to anyone who talked about my weight.

I wasn't getting a lot of action in the bedroom either. My body had changed so much I didn't feel confident letting him see it. I wondered sometimes why nobody told me about this aspect of my life. I didn't think it was possible for my weight to affect my relationship and life so much. Or maybe someone told me and I wasn't hearing. I had always been a slim person so the possibility that my body could expand as it did was confusing to say the least.

When we finally got back in the groove, sex wasn't the same. We had to be mindful of the little one sleeping a few meters away from us. Sometimes he woke up and I had to attend to him, leaving mummy's needs unattended. Then there were times I worried about getting pregnant too soon. You can finally resume sex but you have to worry about not getting pregnant again. And if pregnancy happens, is aborting even an option?

The things I learnt in the year after birthing Boobman are things I will never forget, not only because they tested me to my limit but also because they built me up.

After many months of hating my body and living in denial, I had to come to terms with where I really was and find ways to change my conditioning. The first thing I found that was of real significance was on Instagram. A lady called January started a harsh tag #postpartumbodies and for the first time I read different stories of women who struggled with body changes after birth. These stories gave me the strength I needed to face my own body and accept it exactly as it was.

The first thing I did was stand in front of the bathroom mirror naked. I had decided I would before that morning and I remember feeling nervous because I hadn't looked at my body in a while. As I stood in front of the mirror, it felt like I was looking at someone else. I couldn't relate to my own body. I turned back and saw the folds on my back and sides and I didn't feel disgusted. I actually felt surprised that my body could expand the way it did.

I also offered my body compassion because I had been cruel to it, I hated it and mistreated it. I touched the folds, my tummy and my sagging breasts. As I stood there with my body, I started to feel some level of acceptance. I was seeing my body as mine. I wasn't feeling bad about it and I was realizing that

I am not my body. In that moment, the 'I' and 'My body' felt like two separate people. 'I' was accepting of my body and 'My body' was forgiving of the 'I' for being so mean all those months.

As I started taking care of me, I was better able to take care of my son and my relationship with my husband improved. I wondered how I must have been toward them if I was that mean to myself.

In Eckhart Tolle's book, "A New Earth," he talks about conscious parenting and something he said changed the way I parent Boobman. He said,

"Give your child attention. There are two kinds of attention. One we might call form-based attention. The other is formless attention. Form-based attention is always connected in some way with doing or evaluating. 'Have you done your homework? Eat you dinner. Tidy up your room. Brush your teeth. Do this. Stop doing that. Hurry up. Get ready.' Form-based attention is of course necessary and has its place, but if that's all there is in the relationship with your child, then the most vital dimension is missing and Being becomes completely obscured by doing. Formless attention is inseparable from the dimension of Being. How does it work? As you look at, listen to, touch, or help your child with this or that, you are alert, still completely present, not wanting anything other than that moment as it is. In this way, you are not father or mother. You are the alertness, the stillness, the Presence that is listening, looking, touching, even speaking. You are the Being behind the doing."

After reading this, I started paying attention to how I

was relating to my child. It is easy to get carried away in our world with all its happenings. The children grow up so fast and are gone before we know it. I thought it'd be great if I deliberately practiced formless attention with Boobman. Anytime he comes around and tries to close my laptop I know he is asking for me to be present with him. I see him and I know he knows that I see him. Once I learnt about this, I borrowed my friend the book and showed her the bit about conscious parenting.

The other thing I learnt about conscious parenting is I had to be a mother to myself first. When my baby came along, it was easy to see him as my source of love. It was easy to focus on him as though nothing else was going on in my life. He loved me unconditionally and it was easy to lose myself in his love and become dependent on it. Mothering myself meant trusting myself, it meant loving myself and taking care of myself so I am better able to take care of the vulnerable human that had come into my life.

There is a lot of suffering in our world and most people don't know how to handle their own situations. In these cases, it's the children that suffer. One conscious parent can awaken another parent to his or her own consciousness so that as the children come to the world through us, we are better equipped to honor them on their journey.

I will not 'get it' everyday but each day I am alive I know that my greatest responsibility is to guide this little human that chose me and when it is his turn, he can guide the little human(s) that will choose him too.

17

AWARENESS –

From Believing To Knowing.

"The ultimate value of life depends upon awareness and the power of contemplation rather than upon mere survival." Aristotle.

The first time I heard anything about consciousness was when I read Eckhart Tolle's "Power of Now." It was the year I turned twenty-nine, so when I heard him start off the book with his experience as a twenty-nine-year-old, it was easy to connect as I believed there would be a message in there for me. By the end of the book, which took me eight days to finish, I felt I had found something but I didn't know what it was. I could not articulate it. The book ended with the question, *"how do you know you have surrendered?"* To which Eckhart replied, *"When you no longer need to ask that question"*.

At first I told myself I completely understood all he had talked about. I thought I was ready to change the tone of my relationships and I was beginning my enlightenment journey. It took me three more years to get the message and to bring it to my reality. Prior to when I started living the message, I struggled greatly. I was frustrated because I had all this information I couldn't do anything with. In my mind I always had the perfect response to every situation but when faced with certain circumstances, I would still react in the same old ways I was trying to get rid of.

After my twenty-ninth birthday I stopped going to church. I also stopped praying and reading/listening to Christian materials. Initially I thought it was based on anger. And in my state of being at the time I spent a lot of time attacking Christianity. I thought being Christian had robbed me of all the time I would have used in learning how to be conscious of 'being', and my world.

I went on a desperate search for truth. I read all sorts of materials, I watched all sorts of videos and I attended various seminars to help me figure things out. One seminar that stood out for me was The Landmark Forum. It was a three-day seminar that lasted from ten A.M to nine P.M daily. I was eight months pregnant with my son when I attended the seminar (yeah, I was that desperate).

There were many things I heard during the seminar but my mind wasn't prepared for them at the time so I didn't take any meaningful action. It took another year for the seminar to begin to make sense. One of the main things I heard was about the stories we tell about life. The moderator said that we are always interpreting life through our lenses. So for everything that happens, we interpret it to mean something. By the end of the seminar he was able to convince me that nothing meant anything outside the meaning I give to it.

It takes a degree of mindfulness to not tell stories about one's life's experiences. After the seminar I became a little aware of the stories I told about life but I was powerless to do anything about this awareness. So I committed to more learning about life and growth. I however got frustrated because I was learning a lot of new ways of being but I didn't know how to be that which I needed to be.

A friend gave me "The Secret – Law of Attraction" DVD and that was when something started shifting in my life. Initially I thought the speakers were crazy but they sounded so convincing I decided I was going to try it out. I started learning to attract things that I wanted. I learnt how to make vision boards too and created one for myself. A few years after making my vision board I noticed everything I had on my vision board had happened. I started paying attention to my thoughts and what was manifesting in my world.

After some time of practicing the Law of Attraction I went back to Eckhart Tolle's book 'The Power of Now.' Reading the book again, I felt like I was reading it for the first time. Then a friend gave me another book written by the same author. It was titled 'A New Earth' and by the time I was done reading that book I had a major shift in my perception. It felt as though I had been given keys to understanding my inner and outer world. I was seeing things differently and was getting over my anger at religion. I was also no longer angry with my family, friends, social media or the world. I knew that all was as it should have been and I was ready to be who I was created to be in the world.

As with all learning, I started practicing mindfulness in every area of my life. I also asked a lot of 'why' questions. If something offended me I wanted to know why. If I missed an opportunity I wanted to know why, if someone lied to me and I found out I wanted to know why. I also started remembering all the things that had led me to this place. I had always been a curious being but people around me made me think it was weird and even wrong so I tried to keep all my burning questions inside. Now I was free to ask all the questions I needed to ask but I was no longer asking anyone else, I was asking myself. And I was listening to the voice on the inside that always answered.

The walk grew a bit lonely when I was no longer interested in hanging out with friends. I felt there was something pulling me to spend more time with myself. As I sunk deeper into this journey, different people, books, materials and events started falling off the shelf. What this means is I started finding what I needed to push me forward into this new awareness and learning. I remember Oprah talking about acknowledging when things start to show up to teach you what you need to learn and I remained grateful through it all.

Sometimes I'd share a new insight on Facebook or with my husband because it was too big to keep to myself. It took me a bit to realize that every time I shared something I was just learning, I truncated the learning process. And often I would run into the frustration of not knowing how to defend or explain this new learning. I had to learn to keep my learning quiet. I had to start learning for me, without trying to hurry out to teach someone else something I didn't fully understand.

Many long held beliefs were shaken and I had to unlearn many things, in other to learn and relearn others. One of the biggest lessons for me was death. I used to be so afraid of death. I was afraid of dying and afraid of losing the people I love. It was such a paralyzing fear that I would block thoughts about death from my mind. Yet, death was always around in the news, on social media and from general banter. There was no escaping it. One time I lost a close friend and after a few days of not eating or bathing I decided it was time for me to take care of myself. As I stood in the shower that day, after a few days without a bath, it occurred to me that my friend who died was the one who had escaped the suffering that I was still bound to. And if his ghost could come back to talk to me I was sure he'd want me to stop crying. He would want me to take care of myself. In the last chapter, I write about my new beliefs on death and the purpose I think death serves.

As I grew into this new way of being I found that I could decide my response to every situation. More interesting was I could create the life that I wanted. I found this gnostic site where I learnt about the seven principles of the universe. I spent an entire weekend studying the principles. I read about them on different sites with many relatable examples. By the time I was done I KNEW my life was never going to remain the same. Learning about those principles with everything else I had been exposed to, I knew how to use the keys I had been given from reading Eckhart's books. I spent the next few days in awe of the world. I knew that all of my experiences, both the ones I called good and bad, had brought me to the place I needed to be. I wasn't so eager to teach anybody anything but I knew I had become part of a global awakening and whether I wanted to or not, I was going to help in lighting the fire in others.

The seven principles are:

1. The Principle of Mentalism – All is mind.

2. The Principle of Correspondence – As above, so below.

3. The Principle of Vibration – Motion is manifest in everything.

4. The Principle of Polarity – Everything is dual.

5. The Principle of Rhythm – Everything has a pendulum-like movement.

6. The Principle of Cause and Effect – There is cause for every effect.

7. The Principle of Gender – Masculine and Feminine energies exist in everything.

Attempting to explain any of these principles will take something away from what they mean so I leave them here for you to explore on your own.

I used to struggle with the things I called belief but now I am at peace with the things I KNOW. Awareness for me was the journey from Believing to Knowing. And knowing has little to do with anything I have been taught but everything to do with things

I have realized. Belief is subjective but knowing is complete. As I move forward in my world, I understand I cannot teach anybody anything they don't already know, I can only remind them what they have forgotten. Reminding a person what they have forgotten is lighting the fire that's in them. That fire is in every one of us and by letting my fire burn I show others that it is okay to let theirs burn too.

And when it comes to the god idea, I find that I know there is a Source from which everything flows and is connected to. I think we have called The Source different names through the centuries in a bid to find how to relate with it. I believe this is where the term God originates. All religions are man-made so I feel justified in my suspicion of them all. It is my desire that one day we can trust that every human will find their way and we can stop forcing what we think is the right way down other people's throats.

Everybody has a Knower in them, the more they can relate with the knower, the easier they can expand their awareness and begin to live. And love.

18

PAIN –
The Mother Wound.

"By embracing your mother wound as your yoga, you transform what has been a hindrance in you life into a teacher of the heart."

Phillip Moffitt

PAIN!

We all know it. We all experience it. We talk about it and gravitate towards those we have shared it with. We look for different ways to deal with it. We try desperately to avoid it. Yet, for the most part, we don't know what to do with it.

I have felt pain. Deep, raw, energizing pain. I denied it, cursed it, ran from it and finally embraced it. It was only by embracing it that I was able to release it. I learnt to sit toe to toe with pain and realize that I was not the pain, I was not the hurt, I was not the anger and I was not the hate. I have been to the dark side, I have been to hell, I have met the devil and I have come back with my light.

Have you ever felt the kind of emotional pain that shows up in your physical reality? What I mean is the kind of inner hurt that can cause a chest pain or a headache? I know I have. After years of running from and avoiding pain, I had to embrace it and find that even pain comes with a message.

The average Nigerian female has had painful experiences with her mother. This used to confuse me in my relationship with my mother until I found out it wasn't peculiar to me and there was something I could do about it. In the not so distant past I couldn't talk about my mother without feeling anger or hate. I thought she was my nemesis and there were times I wished death upon her just so I could live in a world where I didn't have to see or hear from her again.

I know I know, terrible of me. How can anyone hate the person that carried her in the womb for nine months? Maybe it wasn't hate, but a deep resentment and frustration for the things I could neither understand nor fix about our relationship.

When I found Bethany Webster, I learnt about something called The Mother Wound and this was the peak of my understanding and healing. She defines The Mother Wound as "*the pain of being a woman passed down through generations of women in patriarchal cultures. And it includes the dysfunctional coping mechanisms that are used to process that pain.*"

She says:

The Mother Wound Includes The Pain Of:

Comparison - Not feeling good enough.

Shame – Consistent background sense that there is something wrong with you.

Attenuation – Feeling you must remain small in order to be loved.

A persistent sense of guilt for wanting more than you currently have.

The Mother Wound Can Manifest As:

- Not being your full self because you don't want to threaten others

- Having a high tolerance for poor treatment from others

- Emotional care taking

- Feeling competitive with other women

- Self-sabotage

- Being overly rigid and dominating

- Conditions such as eating disorders, depression and addictions.

The first time I read this information I knew it was truth. Not only did I relate to every word she wrote, but I had instances flash in my mind as I read through her work. I remembered then, as I remember now, the comparison, the shame, the feeling like I had to play small so that I could keep relationships, the competition with other women, the depression and addictions. I particularly remember blaming my mum for not doing enough to teach me all I needed to know as a girl.

What I understood from Bethany's work was that as daughters we have our mothers' fears unconsciously imprinted on us. So even though I deliberately rejected some of my mother's fears, they became my reality and often showed up in my romantic relationships.

Bethany further writes;

"In our patriarchal, male-dominated culture women are

conditioned to think of themselves as "less-than" and not deserving or worthy. This feeling of "less-than" has been internalized and passed down through countless generations of women. The cultural atmosphere of female oppression puts daughters in a "double bind." Simply put, if a daughter internalizes her mother's unconscious beliefs (which is some subtle form of "I'm not good enough") then she has her mother's approval but has in some way betrayed herself and her potential. However, if she doesn't internalize her mother's unconscious belief in her own limitations but rather affirms her own power and potential, she is aware that her mother may unconsciously see this as a personal rejection. The daughter doesn't want to risk losing her mother's love and approval, so internalizing these limiting, unconscious beliefs is a form of loyalty and emotional survival for the daughter.

It may feel dangerous for a woman to actualize her full potential because it may mean risking some form of rejection by her mother."

I couldn't have put this into words if I tried but I always knew there was something about needing to please my mom in ways I couldn't sustain. I called it 'faking being a good girl.' I knew my dreams were valid but I could never get my mum to see anything good about my writing. One time I told her I was offered a paying job to write and her response, "what do you know that you want to write" stripped me of all confidence, so that I ended up not pursuing the opportunity. I started asking myself what I thought I knew. I was a journaling writer; who would ever pay for that? I needed her to give me something, but you cannot give what you do not have. I don't know how her mother passed The Mother Wound to her and I didn't understand why our relationship was so hard.

A time came that I had to set out to heal The Mother Wound. I didn't identify it as that at the time, but I knew I had to cut contact with my mum if I was going to have a shot at life on my terms. I felt I didn't owe her anything as opposed to what society suggested, about how a mother's sacrifice for her children placed the children in perpetual debt to her. I thought it was her decision to birth me; I didn't have a choice in the matter so no one could ask me to be receptive of her and what I thought was her wickedness toward me. A day came that I moved out of the house. Nobody knew where I was and I moved out because I felt I could no longer live in the same house with my mum. I couldn't explain this to myself let alone someone else but I knew I had to leave in order to grow.

I cut contact with my mum and, by extension, the rest of the family. It was one of the most difficult and empowering times of my life. I realized it was possible that my mother would never understand me. I was tired of trying to be a good girl. I was tired of trying to prove that I needed my own space to grow into the person I knew I was. Sometimes, it felt as though my mother was convinced I was a particular way and attempts to make her see otherwise were futile. The same applied to me; I felt she was stuck in her ways and I was tired of trying to change her or myself to please her. While I was away, all types of accusations were thrown at me from family members. The conclusion was that I was mentally unstable. I think it helped them understand why I would cut contact with my mum and the entire household. I didn't mind too much. I was willing to have them think I was mentally unstable, rather than live in an environment I thought was toxic for me.

I felt the sadness of separation from my family at some point but I also felt I was beginning to heal. I learned that I could be okay even if others didn't understand me. I stopped needing my mum's validation. Understanding myself was satisfying and I knew that the only validation of myself that mattered was my own. Although my mother never rejected me, I knew that I was going to be okay even if she did. I didn't need her approval anymore. I found a deeper part of myself inside me that could sustain and support me on my journey.

Bethany calls estranged daughters, spiritual warriors because *"in a world where women are predominantly expected to stay silent, to cater to the needs of others and where the darker side of mothers is not acknowledged, the experience of estrangement can be an initiation into a new level of awareness that many people never get the opportunity to experience. A space is cleared to allow your light to shine at full radiance."*

I found my light by going where I never thought I could go. Being separate from my family made me realize that on some level we are on our own in the world. We cannot always expect anyone else to support, understand or love us even if they are family. Knowing that one could and should walk their path solo was a huge step in my journey.

By the time I reunited with my mum I was ready for a relationship where I didn't project or allow myself feel small. I was ready to engage her without needing to blame her for my life or take any type of responsibility for hers. I was ready to heal. Healing for me was not just about having a better relationship with my mother. It also meant creating an opportunity for my child to have a good relationship with me where I didn't project upon him my unhealed wounds.

Bethany concludes that, *"The Mother Wound is ultimately not about your mother. It's about embracing yourself and your gifts without shame. We address the mother wound because it is a critical part of self-actualization and saying YES to being the powerful and potent women that we are being called to become. Healing the mother wound is ultimately about acknowledging and honoring the foundation our mothers provided for our lives so that we can then fully focus on creating the unique lives that we authentically desire and know we are capable of creating."*

This bit gave me some comfort as I had sometimes wondered if I was putting blame on my mother. It is ultimately not about her but about the pain passed down from generations of women before her. I call my mum one of my greatest teachers because the pain our relationship woke in me forced me to reach for my highest self in my search for healing. As I started healing my Mother Wound, I knew it was more than just me and my relationship with my child. I knew it was the beginning of the end of something that I would not pass to his generation.

Finally, Bethany makes a list of benefits of healing the Mother Wound. They are:

- Being more fluent and skilled in handling your emotions. Seeing them as a source of wisdom and information.

- Having healthy boundaries that support the actualization of your highest and best self.

- Developing a solid "inner mother" that provides unconditional love, support and comfort to your younger parts.

- Knowing yourself as competent. Feeling that anything is possible, open to miracles and all good things.

- Being in constant contact with your inner goodness and your ability to bring it into everything you do.

- Deep compassion for yourself and other people.

- Not taking yourself too seriously. No longer needing external validation to feel okay.

- Not needing to prove yourself to others.

- Trusting life to bring you what you need.

- Feeling safe in your own skin and a freedom to be yourself.

Healing the Mother Wound was not just helpful to my relationship with my mum and family, it was particularly important for my romantic relationship and how I show up in my world. I haven't gotten it all completely sorted out yet, but I am no longer afraid to live and I will not make myself small on account of any of my relationships. I have permission to live my best life. That permission comes from being born and it doesn't need any outside approval or validation.

I am enough.

19

HAPPINESS –

How To Find Your Happy.

"Happiness doesn't depend on any external condition, it is governed by our mental attitude."

Dale Carnegie.

We live in a world that promotes sadness so when I decided I wanted to be happy it took my brain a while to process that information. I was sitting in my friend's living room listening to her tell me about the day her husband died in that same space where we sat. It was the first time I was hearing a death story that sounded like a love story. She was left with three children to cater for and anyone would feel sorry for her if they heard her story from afar but I couldn't feel sorry for her. I couldn't even cry. Something about her words and the way she told the story made me know that she had something I desired. She was happy. Her children were happy too and her house was filled with love.

I left her house that day and made a decision to be happy. The thought of wanting to be happy scared me. I thought it was crazy that 'happy' could be scary. I called my friend the next day and told her I was scared of 'happy'. She assured me that the fear was normal and encouraged me to stick to my decision to be happy. I did. I went out and bought myself a commitment ring. The ring was to remind me of my decision to be happy. And that was the beginning of my shift in perception regarding happiness. I was better able to understand my fear of 'happy' and dissolve it.

The first time I was in therapy I was also told about finding my happy. My therapist told me all I owed her was happiness. I didn't understand what she meant at the time although I lied that I did. She would often ask, "Are you happy?" to which I'd respond, "Yes" with a smile that was calculated to convince. I think it worked most of the time. I think about that time now and I almost laugh at the thought of trying so hard to convince myself and others that I was happy when it was obvious that I had a lot of unhealed and denied wounds that showed up every time. At this time of the commencement of therapy, I wrongfully carried around the thought that to be happy meant everything in my life had to be going as planned. Since my life was anything but what I wanted it to be at the time, happy was a wish I was probably never going to attain.

When Robin Williams died, it confused me. How could somebody who made other people happy have been so sad during his lifetime? The news made me review my perception about 'happy people.' I wondered if I was ever going to be happy or I would keep pretending until I hurt myself one day.

After my conversation with my dear friend, I realized that the more I declared my happy, the better I got at being comfortable with it. With time I started connecting with people who wanted to know how to be happy. I explained to as many as I could that it was a change in perception that was driven by a decision and commitment to be happy. It also involved allowing yourself feel whatever you were feeling without denying any parts of your feelings. Some thought choosing to be happy meant you have to fight off sadness or negative thoughts and perhaps wear a radiant smile all the time. I didn't struggle with this because I was used to pain and sadness. Suffering used to be my default until I got tired of it and deliberately chose different.

If I were asked how to find one's happy I would say, first of, stop denying what you are feeling. Finding your happy means embracing all parts of yourself. It means laughing when you want to laugh and crying when you want to cry. It means no comparison with another person's state of being. It means taking care of you first so you are better able to take care of others. It means honoring your choices, emotions, decisions and biases. Nothing good ever comes from pretending to be a certain way so that others can feel comfortable around you. You can be happy all by yourself and won't need a person, groups of people or situation to make you happy.

When I made a decision to be happy, I started paying attention to the things that made me happy. I also questioned the things that made me sad. For instance, I found that anytime I had money I was very happy and when I was broke, I was sad. I didn't like that money could alter my state so easily. I started practicing staying happy even when I was broke. I would pay attention to what I did with money when I had it and why it made me happy. I found that it wasn't about what I did with money but the fact that the money was available. Sometimes I would spend needlessly just to prove to myself that money was available. This was the direct opposite of the time where I would spend any money I had until I was back to square one. The former was as dysfunctional as the latter and I needed to quit. I had to learn that I didn't need to spend money just because it was available. I had to come to a place where being financially broke could not determine my happy.

Sometimes dancing helped lift my mood. It still does. There are days when I get the downer bug. Sadness just comes upon me for no reason at all. On those days I put on some music and dance myself back to life and when I don't feel like dancing, I let myself sink into the sadness without needing to judge it. I find that happiness is a decision I can make every day, even on the days when I feel down. The trick for me is to own my downer bug, feel the feelings of sadness, and then when I get tired of it, I can do what I need to do to get myself happy again. And the process isn't really that hard or serious but the outcome. happiness? Now, that's serious business and I do not mess with it.

20

HEALING –
The Myth Of Forgiveness.

'Forgiveness is giving up the hope that the past could have been different.'

Oprah Winfrey.

I like this definition because it doesn't ask me to forget some of the horrible things I experienced.

I struggled with forgiveness because I thought that forgiving someone who had hurt me also meant that I had to forget what he or she had done to me. "Forgive and forget" was a difficult concept for me to grasp. Why did I have to forgive someone that hurt me? What if I did not want to forgive?

I watched Iyanla Vanzant talk about forgiveness once and I bought her book, "21 Days To Forgive Everyone For Everything." However, about fourteen days into the practice that was supposed to span twenty-one days, I lost interest in the book. I figured it was not going to work for me. Iyanla had many interesting stories about how she learnt to forgive different people in her life, but in my reality I was struggling. Okay, I wasn't struggling; I just didn't want to forgive anyone.

I thought forgiveness made me weak. I thought about the Christian boy I had dated who had stolen from me. I shared my bankcard details with him because . . . well, love. It had been easy to trust him because he was a youth leader in church and we were having a 'Christian relationship.' You know those types of relationships where you save sex for marriage? It turned out he'd been a fraud, stealing from me for months, without my having a clue. How do you begin to forgive that?

I thought about the friend and business partner who

duped me, and how she threw my past in my face when I confronted her. How do you forgive that? Shouldn't the right thing to do in such a case be to drag that kind of person to the courts and get back your money?

I thought about my ex-boyfriends. I knew I still hated some of them. I was sure I'd never be able to forgive them. They had caused me too much pain and now I was just supposed to forgive and forget?

I thought forgiveness was overrated. I was not going to do it. And what was more, I was also going to enact revenge on all these people (insert evil laugh).

I heard that healing involved forgiveness. And I wanted to heal. I wanted the pain, anger, and disappointment to go away. So instead of asking why people were hurting me I started asking what they were teaching me. Remember that pain comes with a message?

The most difficult times in my life have brought the most important lessons. It has been the same way with the most difficult people in my life. The people who I thought abused me were the people who taught me my greatest lessons. Yes, he was a thief, but the boyfriend I didn't want to forgive because he stole from me, was the person who taught me about desperation. My friend who attacked me with the 'shame story' I shared with her, was the person who taught me about how quickly and easily people could turn on you. These experiences as well as many others taught me something about human behavior and life. That cannot be a bad thing, so how could I possibly stay angry at that?

And so, I changed my mind about forgiveness. I began to think that it was cool to forgive all of these people. And I asked some of them for forgiveness too – an exercise that wasn't as weird as I imagined. It was freeing. It brought peace with it. The day I sent messages out to everyone I was not speaking with, I didn't feel it was a hard thing to do. It felt like the right thing to do. It freed me and even when some chose not to respond to my message, I knew it was enough that I had reached out. I, however, also learnt that it was possible to forgive a person without needing to tell them you had forgiven them. In the same vein, it is possible to forgive yourself on another person's behalf without needing them to validate that forgiveness.

Healing meant owning the disowned parts of myself. It is actually easy to recognize the disowned parts of yourself. All you need to do is pay attention to the things you complain about the most in other people. It is very obvious in the people closest to you. I learnt how to own my disowned parts by paying attention to the various behaviors of my mother and my husband, which I used to always complain about. They showed me the parts of me I was running away from, and when I owned every part of me, it was easy to stop projecting on them. It was easy to stop blaming them.

I realize I am enough. I am worthy. I am grateful for all the experiences life has given me to bring me to this place. I no longer judge others and myself. I believe everything that happens in my life serves a purpose and, until the purpose becomes clear to me, not knowing what it serves is also enough. Healing means accepting everything that is without judgment. It also means letting my inner child know that she is safe and has always been.

I am at peace.

21

FEMINA SPEAKS –

Finding My Voice.

"Your work is going to fill a large part of your life, and the only way to be truly satisfied is to do what you believe is great work. And the only way to do great work is to love what you do. If you haven't found it yet, keep looking. Don't settle. As with all matters of the heart, you'll know when you find it. And, like any great relationship, it just gets better and better as the years roll on. So keep looking until you find it. Don't settle."

Steve Jobs.

In 2011, I decided I wanted to be a Nigerian Oprah. This 'Nigerian Oprah' dream was flawed for several reasons. First, when you decide to be someone else, you give up yourself, completely defeating the idea of authenticity. Also, I had never hosted a talk show in my life. I figured it was easy since Oprah did it so well but in reality, it wasn't. It could not have been.

In analyzing my flawed dream, I realized it wasn't that I really wanted or needed to host a talk show; I just wanted to help other people. I didn't understand how to go about this and Oprah was the closest model of what I wanted to achieve, hence my Nigerian Oprah dream.

For a long time, I was voiceless. I thought I had a lot to say but I felt like a second-class citizen. I felt like an inferior being. My world taught me that as a woman I was somehow disadvantaged. Anytime I spoke about the things I cared about, I felt that what I had to say wasn't really important. It didn't matter.

But I grew tired of playing small. I grew tired of hiding parts of me that were seeking expression. I grew tired of the silence so I found my voice. Femina Speaks literally means, "woman speaks."

Sometimes I remember my teenage and young adult self and I laugh. I was a naïve girl who went about acting wise. I see a version of myself in many teenage and young adult females I meet. And I want to hug them and say, *"It's okay to be confused, it's okay to not know what you want to do with your life and it's okay to not pretend like you do."*

Femina Speaks started as a radio show and vlog. The focus was on abuse against women, but it was really my way of speaking up about what I called the abuse I had experienced. I spoke about emotional abuse, mental health, domestic violence and the importance of seeking help. I believe a lot of women related to it easily because we are sold the victim story early in life. But about six months into hosting the radio show, I stopped. I felt something was missing. I also felt I had not healed enough to be able to help others on their journey.

I took time off everything and focused on me. I embarked on a journey to self. I wanted to know Ese, what she liked, who she was, and why she existed on the earth. This journey is the reason I have written this book. It is also the reason I have clarity on my life's purpose and what Femina Speaks is about.

Getting to know myself meant accepting myself fully - flaws and all. By accepting myself fully, I was able to accept others too. I also became clear on what I wanted my life's experiences to be. I no longer needed to be Oprah. I now knew I could simply be Ese, and that felt good. I found my voice and I decided to use it. More than that, I decided to help every young adult female I meet find her voice. Femina Speaks is for the young lady who is confused about life, love, purpose and what it all means. Femina Speaks exists to guide her to asking the right questions. Femina Speaks is my permission to speak; my permission to live my message knowing that I am indeed enough.

Still, for a long time I didn't feel I was worthy of my message. Despite everything I had learned and unlearned, I still found myself doubting myself. I thought I needed someone to continually affirm me. I thought I needed permission to be the person I was created to be. I thought I needed help in learning how to help young women. But this fight against external affirmation was not new to me. I had been down that road before. I tapped into my past feelings of self-realization, and took on the bravery to help these young women in the best way I knew how. I talked with them and to them. I didn't stop. And as I continued, I found that it actually came naturally to me. I always saw the young me in these girls so cutting through the different layers of personalities and addressing the girl in the girl, became second nature.

Femina Speaks has started as a mentorship platform. I am not sure about the modus operandi but I know I am ready to help the young girls I call sisters. I also know that if I have to do this for the rest of my life, it will be a life well lived.

On the flip side of Femina Speaks is Making Tomorrow's Gentlemen Today (**MTGT**). I first got this idea when I started thinking about boys and how confused they must be about what it means to be male. We are so focused on helping the woman that we forget that men need help too.

MTGT is a mentorship platform for boys and young

men. It exists to remove stigmatization around men seeking help. We cannot empower women and ignore the fact that women share the earth with men and will have to exist alongside daily.

On earth, massive opportunities abound for both men and women. In some cases, men thrive more than women, and in other cases women thrive more than men. No one gender is more important than the other.

MTGT is therefore balance for Femina Speaks. I tried to get someone else to run with this idea. I figured that being a man, he was best equipped for things that have to do with men. But my friend reminded me that even though we want men to step up to the plate and raise boys, it is mainly women who raise these boys. The dysfunction we see in both men and women can also be corrected and avoided by women. So I have taken **MTGT** as part of my work.

A few young men reached out to me concerning different things like masturbation, work life, confusion about life's choices, depression, and needing someone to talk to. I handled the situations the best way I knew how but I didn't feel 'enough' to offer them the help they needed. I thought they had to reach out to fellow men who would better understand them and offer sound advice. I know now that I only thought that way because I was unprepared at the time. But I am ready now. I will not have all the answers; however, I am a great connector and find that I can steer people where they need to go to find the right questions. Sometimes, this is all people need, and it is enough.

I have the best job in the world.

22

PURPOSE – Why I'm Here.

"So many people are looking for it: their Big Life Purpose. Becoming you is your purpose. You are the very purpose of your existence. Realizing what lights your fire and floats your boat – that's your life purpose. What else could it be? If it gives you true joy (not the seemingly happy high that is fleeting, but the reliable, always-there kind of satisfaction) to rock that guitar, to make people laugh, to discover the world, to make things a little more beautiful wherever you go, to feed. To stir it up, to clean it up, to execute the plan, to bank the cash, to be a compassionate citizen, to explore nonstop, or purely to seek pleasure … then, that's your life's purpose! Your life purpose is what you say it is. Who could tell you otherwise?"

Danielle LaPorte.

A lot has been said about purpose but enough cannot be said. I declared my purpose for the first time a few months after I turned thirty-two. I remember talking about it at the maiden edition of Mind Experience seminar and someone asked if I was serious about only just realizing my purpose. The first thing I learnt about purpose is that it was not as complicated as I thought it would be. Purpose meant asking the questions: who am I? Why am I here?

Am I here to eat, sleep, sex, cohabit, reproduce, work, and die? Is it possible that my existence means more than that cycle? And if it goes beyond that, how do I figure out how to beat the rat-race and live a life that's worthy of my time on the earth?

The first time I held a job was during my chamber attachment. I was going to a law firm as a law student and I had the opportunity to see what being a lawyer truly looked like. It did not take long for me to know that I didn't want that to be my life. I then worked at a media house as a sales officer but I didn't like that job either. After I quit my third job, I realized that the problem was not the kind of jobs I had done, but the structure of work that those jobs involved. Going to a place every day to sit behind a desk from nine A.M to five P.M was not how I wanted to spend my time. It felt like torture. I was a curious restless being. Putting me behind a desk in a room was like caging a bird.

One of the early books I read on 'purpose' was Rick Warren's "The Purpose-Driven Life." It had a forty-day exercise that I never got around to completing. I judged myself as simply being unable to commit. But now, I realize I had simply rebelled against the idea of anyone getting me to do anything and giving me a timeline to do it. Added to that, I also think there might have been a layer of fear.

"What if I complete it and find my purpose, what do I do with that?"

The second time I tried to figure out my purpose was when I listened to Barbara Sher talk about doing what you love. In her book "Wishcraft", she uses different exercises to help you remember things you loved doing as a kid. She believes the things a person loved as a kid are the things they are passionate about. She says the things you love doing are an indication of your DNA telling you what your passion is.

Upon completing one of Barbara's exercises, I found that I loved writing (I kept a journal since I learned to write), I loved singing (performing in front of my mirror had always been a thing), I loved movies and playing pretend, and I loved learning by trying. I am one of those people who learn better by experience. I am big on experiences. In fact, I am in life for the experience, and there are things I have done just for the thrill of the experience.

I once went skydiving, I tried acupuncture, and I learned to ride a horse in four days. I assumed these were things that people generally loved doing but I was wrong. My therapist brought this to my attention one day while I was telling her about the structures I built with Lego. When I bought the Lego box, I told myself I was buying it for my son. I realize I bought it for myself but used my son as my cover-up because I thought I was too old to build Lego structures.

The day I went skydiving, nobody in my family knew about it. I knew they were going to discourage me so I planned and executed before ever telling anyone about it. The jump was in Cambridge and I lived in London at the time. I left the house early to make my trip to Cambridge and I was feeling all types of excited as I got on the train for the trip. I had my journal with me so I wrote down how I was feeling on the train to Cambridge, on my way to the skydiving site, and while I waited for my turn to dive.

October 1, 2013.

Beginnings are always awesome. Being alone on this train is giving me time I need to think. This music by Pink is putting me in a happy place. The landscape outside is showing me a picture of what peace should be.

I am actually going skydiving today. Hehehe. That's skydiving off my bucket list. I am thankful for opportunities. I initially didn't know the dive was outside London so I have spent over 70quid on transport to Cambridge. 30quid for the cab to King's Cross station and 42quid return ticket to Cambridge.

Paid a cab to the dive site as well so this means money I planned for pictures is gone. How to raise money for pictures? This experience needs to be captured.

Guess what though? I have been able to get over 100quid from friends in Nigeria. Thankful. Weird how I remained happy and thankful despite how the situation looked. Maybe that's why it all got sorted.

And now despite making this journey and raising the money, jumps have been paused because of the wind. I still believe I will make the jump today. I strolled out and spoke to that wind like Jesus did on the boat with his disciples and despite the fact that they haven't called us, I know we will jump.

WE here is me and this nice family I have been talking with and observing. A mum over 60 with her son and daughter. I'm still trying to determine who the older child is. I suspect the guy's younger.

While I was watching the first and second group land, it was so beautiful. The plane took off and disappeared into the clouds, next thing, we saw what seemed like stains in the sky, then images began to emerge and when they were visible enough it seemed as though they were going to crash into the ground but it was a soft landing instead.

Looking forward to my turn… 2:12PM.

A few hours later we made our jump. I remember the experience like it happened yesterday. It was the same way I spoke to myself about learning to ride a horse in a week. I did it in four days but before ever getting on the horse I said, *"By this time next week I will ride a horse like the man I saw riding at the beach."*

My therapist said, *"it seems your purpose is to experience life and teach others how to do the same."* And it made perfect sense. It was an 'aha!' moment for me and pushed me to start thinking about the things that drove me.

I would not spend a lot of money on cloths, shoes or even cars, but I could spend my last Naira on an experience like travel or learning to ride a horse. Amongst my friends, I was always the one who wanted to experience things just for how they made me feel.

One time we went to Thorpe Park in the UK and my friends were afraid to get on some rides because they were "scary rides". I was eager to get on all the scary rides. Someone called me an adrenaline junkie. I think a better term would be "feeler." I love experiences because I am a feeling person and I want to feel. My therapist said just by listening to me talk about my many experiences she was already trying new things out. She said she used to be one for experiences but gave it all up at a point in her life, but after talking to me, she was considering picking it back up again.

She wasn't the first person to say that to me. A lot of people in my life say I motivate them to try out new things. It became clear to me that I was already living my purpose. I was already experiencing life and inspiring others to experience life, too.

Going forward, I want to fill my life with experiences that push me forward in my evolution. I want to grow spiritually, physically, and emotionally as I visit places and meet people that stimulate my life's experience. I want to turn strangers into friends and show them how satisfying life can be whether you have the millions or not. I want to live life fully and, by doing this, show others that they can live fully too.

These are exciting times. I am happy to be alive in this time. I have found my purpose and I will continue to live it until this physical form expires in what we call death.

I think the ultimate purpose of life is to live. I am living until I die.

23

DEATH –

A Reminder To Love Now.

"When your time comes to die, be not like those whose hearts are filled with fear of death, so that when their time comes they weep and pray for a little more time to live their lives over again in a different way. Sing your death song, and die like a hero going home."

Tecumseh

I used to be afraid of death. I didn't want to die and I didn't want my family to die. I'd say prayers like, *"Lord, please protect me and my family."* As though the rest of the earth didn't need protecting. I thought death was a bad thing and it brought sadness every time. I thought death could happen to everyone else but me because I prayed against it a lot. It was denial. I started seeing death differently after I lost a friend.

His name was Ush and he had just gotten married to his pregnant partner. Ush was the kind of guy that was everybody's friend. In school, he played basketball and had this 'fine boy' swag. I was living outside Nigeria at the time he died but I had seen him a few weeks prior. I even chatted to him on BBM on the morning of his wedding.

When my younger brother called me one morning to say Ush had died, I thought he was mistaken. He said my friend had been shot at, in his own home. I hung up and opened my BBM chat records. I sent a message. And another one. Then a 'ping'. Another ping. Three pings, and then I got another call from a former classmate. She said Ush was killed. I called mutual friends to find out if it was true. They all confirmed Ush was shot.

I went to his Facebook page. Condolence messages had filled his timeline. I thought about the last time I saw him, I thought about his wife, his unborn child, his mother and his close friends. I sat on the floor of my house and burst into tears. I was screaming like I had a knife in my back. I couldn't stop crying. I felt my head getting hot like it was going to explode. I paced the house with my eyes filled with tears. I was talking to myself. "How can this be? I just saw him when I was in Nigeria. He just got married. Who could want to kill Ush? Did they know how sweet he was? Did he beg them? What happened in Warri?"

Over the next week I was a wreck. I didn't eat and I didn't clean my house. I hardly had baths during this period. When I eventually did, I let the shower run until I had the strength to climb out of the tub.

During this time, I would always leave the TV on even though I had stopped watching it. I only needed to hear sounds. I needed to hear voices in my immediate space. A friend finally showed up at my house one day, despite my insistence that I wanted to be alone.

She helped me clean up the place, and then she cooked me a meal. She offered some condolence messages but I wasn't hearing her. After food I went to bed and had restful sleep for the first time since I heard the news of Ush. When I woke up, I started thinking about everything that had happened the days before.

I knew it was time to resume lectures and living. I started going to class again and returning to my old self. From this pain I drew a lesson, too. I learned that human beings will adapt, evolve, and grow no matter what happens. When people die, the people they leave behind will feel sadness for a while and then they will have to move forward somehow. Why then did I get all sad and hurt over the period of time I did if I was going to come out of it and be my playful self again?

This was the beginning of my new relationship with death. I thought about my family, the small unit of my parents and siblings. What would I do if my parents or siblings died tomorrow? What would they do if I died? The same things I did when my friend died – live in and with the sadness, and eventually move on. I figured that if death was inevitable, wasn't 'now' the time to start talking more about death?

Isn't 'now' the only time to love others, before they die? Why do we treat each other like we hate each other only for one person to die and then we are filled with regret? No one knows what happens after death but we can be here now, while we are alive. Why do we not choose this instead?

And is death the end? Does it mean that we cease to exist? Before I answer that I'd like to share something that happened when my friend lost her younger brother.

When I heard her brother had died, I went to visit her, in the company of my cousin. My friend had been crying so much and when she managed through her grief to tell us about how her brother died, I saw in her the picture of me grieving Ush's death.

I remembered all the crying and hopelessness I had felt. I thought I understood what she was feeling but instead of getting on the floor to cry with her I started trying to tell jokes.

This was completely inappropriate and it took me many years and a lost friendship to realize this. Thinking back, I must have been trying to escape the sadness in the room and on another level I thought that by making jokes I could get her and others to feel better. It didn't work at all, and that was the last time I saw that friend.

These days when people experience death, the best I can do if I go around them is to sit with them in quiet or ask how they are feeling. I do not offer condolences or anything like that. I do not try to make them feel better, because they have the right to own their sadness and it is not in my place to dismiss it on their behalf.

I do not think that death is the end, though. I think the life force in every living thing cannot die. I believe that what happens at death is an expiration of the body. When the body goes, the life force continues to exist and can return in another form. Why death hurts is because we will never see the person again, at least not in the form we know them. I also believe that when they appear in another form they will not recognize the ones they left behind and the ones they left behind will not recognize them. This is perhaps what gives death that ring of finality.

For me, death therefore serves as a reminder to love, now. Death tells me I will not be here with these experiences forever. Along with telling me to love now, death challenges me to live while I am alive. It tells me to write this book, sing my own song, tell my story, love hard, give without expectation, receive freely and never fall to the level of merely existing.

I am no longer afraid of death. I know it will come for me and for the people I love. I hope that as we evolve, we grow to understand death. I also hope that we get to the point where we do all we can do today so that if tomorrow is when we die, then we die like heroes going back home.

WRITING THIS BOOK

The idea for a book didn't come as a suggestion by well-meaning friends or strangers. It came from within me. I WANTED TO WRITE A BOOK. I wanted a part of me to be left in the world, as part of my footprints.

But it took me three years to do this. I know now that the reason it took me this long was the fear of achieving that dream of putting my words out in the universe. I probably thought, *"Who am I, to actually write a book – what do I have to say that means anything?"* and this fear had not come from nowhere.

When I started telling the people around me that I wanted to write a book, I got responses that ranged from, *"you ought to have achieved something with your life before you think of writing a book about your life,"* to *"what do you want to write that you think people will want to read?"*

There were also the ones who thought I was a fantastic writer and needed to write a book. The problem was that they believed in me far more than I believed in myself.

I started writing the book after I got encouragement

from another writer. I watched various writing advice videos by authors. I joined Nanowrimo and did their thirty-day writing challenge. That was the first time I completed the first draft of the book. The challenge was in November and by March of the next year I decided to edit the book and make plans to publish. Editing the book felt like rewriting it, and by the third day of editing I deleted the entire thing. I didn't feel that it was good enough, or that I had marshaled my points clearly enough.

I started the book afresh and this time it was clearer but very angry. Writing whipped up all types of emotions and thoughts that I had long buried. I wrote about things I hadn't fully understood. I wrote about people I believed had hurt or abused me. I got in full victim mode and let it rip.

This time I got a copywriter to edit the book. When the book came back I felt like something was still missing. I didn't look at the manuscript for a few days. By the time I started reading it I knew I still had a lot of work to do. A few months and some tweaking later, I sent it out to the publishers.

The book came back a few days later with plenty highlighted pages and a letter saying I needed to change a lot of things in it to protect identities or get release letters from everybody I wrote about in the book. I didn't even use real names but like I said, it was an angry book and so I understood what the publishers meant. I wasn't pleased though, because

I realized that all the re-working would mean it was not going to be published any time soon.

A few days later, after my initial displeasure, I felt some relief that the book had not seen the light of day. Something in me realized that it wasn't even complete. I was ready to do what needed doing, but this time I was in no hurry. I played with the thought of making a fictional book so that I could mask certain events but that thought soon disappeared. It was my story and I was going to own it.

I wrote another editor and asked if she could edit my book. She replied and asked a few questions about my book. As I read her response, I knew I had found my editor. I drew another outline and started thinking about the book you hold in your hand. I knew I could tell my story without making the focus anyone else but me. I remembered something I heard in "Eat, Pray, love" about seeing everyone you meet as teachers, and everything that happens as lessons.

I finally get it. The events that happened in my life that led me where I am were all necessary to bring me to this place. I deleted the angry book and wrote a new one with the outline I came up with.

This is the third & final draft of NAKED.

If you want to write a book, go ahead and write it. The permission you need to write a book *(or do anything your heart wants)* is already yours. You got the permission by being born. So, just do it.

THE END.

ABOUT THE AUTHOR

Ese is an attorney and author.

She is a humanist and a citizen of planet earth.

After decades of sleepwalking through life, she is learning that life is a journey, all her experiences are lessons, and people she meets along the way are teachers.

One of her biggest likes is mindfully experiencing life and her biggest dislike is writing bios.

You can connect with via email at esewalter@gmail.com

REFERENCE

- African Culture and the Ongoing Quest for Excellence," Maulana Karenga
- Brene Brown – The power of vulnerability.
- Dr. William James - Single mothers raising sons in a fatherless home.
- John Dermartini - The Breakthrough Experience.
- Eckhart Tolle – A New Earth.
- Eckhart Tolle – The Power of Now.
- Iyanla Vanzant - 21 Days to forgive everyone for everything.
- Rick Warren – Purpose driven life.
- Barbara Sher – Wish Craft.